MANAGE. LEAD. TRANSFORM.

A Project Manager's Guide to Reducing Project Timelines by 50% or More.

By
SHAKEEL AKHTAR AND AYESHA HAKIM
www.p3alphaconsulting.com

Copyright © Shakeel Akhtar and Ayesha Hakim, 2017
All rights reserved.

FREE BONUS

MLT framework MindMap

A Mindmap of the 15 processes of the MLT framework

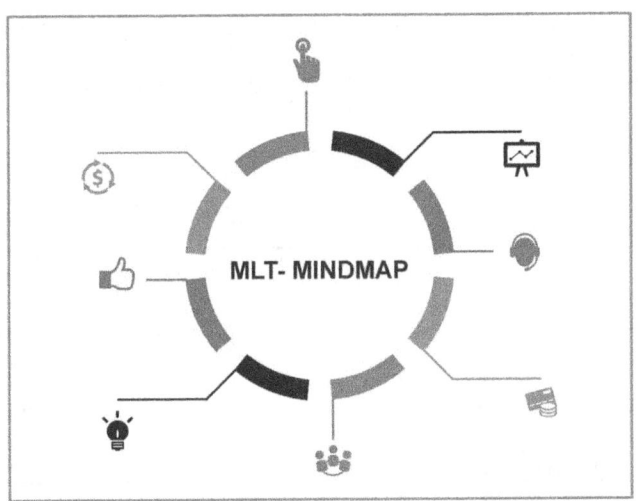

Visit the link below link to get free bonus.

http://www.p3alphaconsulting.com/bonus/

CONTENTS

"Take up one idea. Make that one idea your life - think of it, dream of it, live on that idea. Let the brain, muscles, nerves, every part of your body, be full of that idea, and just leave every other idea alone. This is the way to success."

– Swami Vivekananda

Free Bonus iii

Preface vi

Acknowledgements ix

About the Authors 1

    Chapter 1 Introduction: Why projects fail? 3

    Chapter 2 Defining Structure 15

Part 1: Manage **25**

Chapter 3   Own Your Tasks 26

Chapter 4   Know a task from a project 32

Chapter 5   Break down your tasks 38

Chapter 6   Avoid Multitasking 45

Chapter 7   Prioritize your Tasks 54

Chapter 8   Schedule your Buzz 59

Chapter 9   Report your tasks right 65

Chapter 10   From Managing to Leading 73

Part 2: Lead 79

Chapter 11   Lead right 80

Chapter 12   Set Priorities 85

Chapter 13   Promote a culture of recognizing great work . 90

Chapter 14   Facilitate Great Work 97

Chapter 15   Eliminate Bad Meetings 108

Chapter 16   From Leading to Transforming 115

Part 3 – Transform 119

Chapter 17   Establish a rallying cry 120

Chapter 18   Align Strategic Initiatives 126

Chapter 19   Schedule Health Checkups 132

Chapter 20   Conclusion: From Transforming to Transcending 137

Free Bonus 145

PREFACE

"A bad system will beat a good person every time"

— W Edwards Deming

As a husband-and-wife team of Project Management Consultants, we have written this book as a guide for Project Managers to reduce their project timelines by 50% or more. It is a fact that projects get delayed regularly and sometimes fail. The average IT project is delayed by 222%, as per the Standish report. This means a 2-week project could take more than 6 weeks to complete, and a 1-year project could take more than 3 years to complete. With great improvements in the capabilities of project management software and the amazing productivity features of these tools, you would think that the trend would change, right? Unfortunately, the trend is getting worse.

MANAGE. LEAD. TRANSFORM.

You, the project manager, are getting frustrated because you are at the forefront of this crisis. You see tasks delayed on a daily basis. You feel, every task, almost every task is being delayed. You could be a PMP, or in the process of becoming one. You thoroughly know all the processes of all the knowledge areas of Project Management Knowledge of Book (PMBoK). You have also trained yourself in Agile, Scrum, Kanban, RAD, and Six Sigma. You know what to do, and have tried a few things out, but nothing seems to be working.

You have come to the right place. In this book, we have taken years of our project management experience and perfected a framework called MLT – Manage, Lead, and Transform. The MLT framework is built from thousands of hours of our innovation in the area of effectiveness, and condenses into 15 processes that work right off the bat. With our processes, you will start seeing results within a week. Our processes have delivered a 100% success rate, and we guarantee your projects will start turning around as you start implementing one process after another.

The second advantage is that you do not need to learn any difficult concepts like earned value management or learn any SPI/CPI calculations or learn how to make burn down charts.

The third advantage is the visibility that you get when your projects turn around, and you get noticed within your organization. With that visibility, your career will transform, and

MANAGE. LEAD. TRANSFORM.

you will be given the opportunity to lead bigger projects and bigger teams.

What are you waiting for? Let's get started!

ACKNOWLEDGEMENTS

"In the end, though, maybe we must all give up trying to pay back the people in this world who sustain our lives. In the end, maybe it's wiser to surrender before the miraculous scope of human generosity and to just keep saying thank you, forever and sincerely, for as long as we have voices."

—Elizabeth Gilbert

We have worked with so many teams on so many projects that it is quite impossible to thank everyone who contributed to our ideas, helped with our experiments, and guided us during our challenges. Having said that, we have come across excellence during our careers, and that excellence has rubbed on us. For that, we would like to thank Bill Gunderson, Brent Brown, Cathy Savinsky, Chandra Dyamangoudar, Dale Hite, David Fairclough, Debra Brown, Dinesh Deshmukh, Helen Drexler, Jane Hamerle, John Wilson, Scott Porter, and Taj Haslani.

We also have benefitted tremendously from all the subject matter on not just project management but also on leadership, processes, and technology. Many times we thought our individual ideas to be very original only to find out later on that these ideas were documented, tested, and implemented a long time back. The thought leaders whose work has influenced our thinking are David Allen, Marshall Goldsmith, Michael Bungay Stanier, Patrick Lencioni, Peter Senge, Scott Berkun, and Tim Ferriss.

While writing this book, we have received tremendous support and inspiration from our daughter Heba. Her goofiness combined with her worldly wisdom was very helpful during the writing of this book.

We would also like to thank our parents and our family members for their best wishes.

ABOUT THE AUTHORS

"I have not yet learned to use our television DVR. One of the points of marriage is that you split labor. In the olden days that meant one hunted and one gathered; now it means one knows where the tea-towels are kept and the other knows how to program the DVR, for why should we both have to know?"

– Elizabeth Alexander

Shakeel Akhtar and Ayesha Hakim are the co-founders of the project management consulting company, *P3Alpha Consulting*. *P3Alpha Consulting* provides innovative consulting in successful project delivery, setup/enhancement of PMOs, and recovery of troubled projects.

Shakeel Akhtar, PMP, CSM, is a highly effective and dynamic senior program director with high emotional intelligence needed to inspire large teams to deliver. He has more than fifteen years of experience in project management in three major business sectors: Healthcare, Telecommunications and Financial industry. He has spent the last several years developing project management offices (PMOs) and training project managers. He is also an accomplished leader, communicator, and public speaker. He is passionate about coaching, mentoring, and training project managers to successfully deliver complex projects while advancing their careers. He has improved effectiveness and productivity in small, mid-size to large organizations resolving their unique challenges. He is an expert at managing technology change by focusing on people first and processes/methodology second. In his free time, Shakeel loves to blog on life and work at www.itsonelife.com

Ayesha Hakim MBA, PMP, is an accomplished project manager and public speaker holding project management and Agile related certifications. Ayesha brings vision, leadership, and strategic thinking to align portfolios, programs, and projects to the strategic initiatives of the client companies. Her thought leadership in project management is par excellence and has benefitted every program and project that she has successfully delivered. Ayesha possesses detailed knowledge and experience in many analysis tools and techniques. Her experience covers many industries including Healthcare, Software, Banking and Retail. She is passionate about helping project managers develop processes to build efficient teams than can seamlessly deliver straightforward and complex projects. She has also successfully set up project management offices (PMOs) locally and internationally to help mid-size to large corporations. She has helped organizations smoothly transition from waterfall to agile delivery successfully.

CHAPTER 1

INTRODUCTION: WHY PROJECTS FAIL?

"Success has many fathers, but failure is an orphan"

The Situation – Monday Morning Crisis

Imagine it is a regular Monday morning - nothing special or significant about this particular Monday. You arrive at your office, and as you walk in, you glance around to find that your entire team is in the office and is seemingly busy. Since, it is a typical Monday morning and you have umpteen things to take care of - meetings to attend, emails to go through, and phone calls to make, you get started on your tasks. You get busy, oblivious to the fact that statistically speaking, less than 10% of your seemingly busy team may be working on a task that is not the right task to do at that point in time by that team member. Forget about your team, you may not be working on the right task for that Monday morning. How is that possible?

According to a Gallup Poll, only 32% of the workforce is engaged, which means almost 2 out of 3 employees are disengaged. The work habits of these employees, according to Gallup surveys, are to do "the bare minimum and to kill time while constantly thinking about lunch or their next break." When 2 out of 3 employees are not working with a sense of urgency and purpose, the tasks are not getting done on time. When and if these tasks do get done, it is unlikely that they will be completed to a high quality.

So, who gets to pick up the delayed tasks and try to make the deadlines? Who gets to fix the poor-quality work done by the disengaged employees? Yes, you guessed right - engaged employees. Many studies show that three-fourths of these engaged employees will be working on managing crises at any point of time. Most of the time, disengaged employees may have caused these crises by not proactively identifying risks. Risks that could have been managed when they showed up and not when they blew up. Managing crises is not the right way of doing tasks. It can cause burnout as well as low quality work.

According to Stephen Covey, most work falls under one of the four quadrants, as explained in his book, "The 7 habits of highly effective people." The four quadrants are as follows:

1. Quadrant 1 – Important and Urgent.
2. Quadrant 2 – Important and Not Urgent.
3. Quadrant 3 – Not Important and Urgent.
4. Quadrant 4 – Not important and Not Urgent.

The best quality work is done when working on Quadrant 2 tasks - important but not urgent. 68% of the workforce (disengaged) could be either working in Quadrant 3, at best or at worst, in Quadrant 4.

24% (three-fourths of engaged) of the workforce could be working on tasks that are in Quadrant 1. That is 92% of the entire workforce that could be doing tasks that are not the right tasks at the right time.

So, what % of your team could be working on the right task on your typical Monday morning? What about you? Are you putting out a fire on that Monday morning or scanning your email to see which fire to put out of the many fires that have shown up in your inbox.

Now, what does the disengagement of your team have to do with your projects? Let's get into it a little deeper.

Impact of Not Working on Right Task

What is the impact of not getting the right task done by the right person at the right time, most of the time? If your company is a project-based company, where your company makes money by finishing projects on time, then that's where you look. You take a look at your projects to see how many projects fail. You could tell that you never delivered your projects on time and neither were you late. That may sound very smart, but at the end of the day, you had negotiated and renegotiated your project deadlines so that your projects were never called late and at the same time were never on time.

We hope that you do not take that tactic but seriously look at the projects that you have been associated with and worked on in some capacity. How many of your recent projects have failed? Maybe, your company's criteria for success may be different from others and so let's take a look at some criteria for project success.

Project Success Is Not Common

For the numerous types of projects that are undertaken in the world, the majority fail. Before unpacking this statement, let us define what failure is. Failure in its simplest terms is not achieving the desired result within a set of pre-determined parameters.

With this definition of project success criteria, if we look around, then we may find more projects that can be tagged as failed rather than successful. However, there is a distinction that needs to be drawn here as to the types of projects we are talking about, because there are many types of projects. "Inventing a light bulb" type project will not be part of this discussion because Edison found thousands of ways of not making the light bulb. Not a failure! Similarly, "building a house" type project will not be part of this discussion for multiple reasons; the primary among them is that we have thousands of years of experience building houses, and even so, we do not see buildings fall down on a regular basis. In the former type of projects, success is not guaranteed, and in the latter type of projects, success is common. In addition to these, there are Happiness Projects, Habit Projects, Husband Projects (yes, there is a book called Husband Project), etc., which we will ignore in this book for obvious reasons.

If we take out the projects that are on the opposite sides of the spectrum, where on one side there are projects that no one has ever done before and on the other side are the projects that have been done hundreds or thousands of times before, we are still left with a large number of projects. These projects have some basic characteristics in common as shown below.

- Desired outcome that can be defined and understood.
- Constraints like time, cost and quality.

Of these projects, let's take a subset, IT projects, for the sole reason that there have been extensive studies done on these types of projects.

The Standish Group has been collecting data on IT projects for many years, and their recent findings are no different from the earlier ones. It is the same story being repeated over and over again every year. Here are some of the highlights of the report

- Average success rate is 16.2%, and only 9% for large companies.
- >250 Billion Dollars are spent on IT projects in the United States, and the bigger problem is the opportunity cost of failed projects that could go in Trillions of dollars.
- The average overrun is 222% of the original time estimate
- High % of executives believe that there are more project failures now than five or ten years previously.

The IT projects are just a sample of the total projects. 16% success rate in IT projects may be low for non-IT projects and even if there is a 3 times better rate in other types of projects, the success rate of projects could be still less than 50%. So, we need to acknowledge the fact that the majority of projects fail.

Published Causes of Project Failure

Now that we have established that project failure is common among projects that have a desired outcome within a set of pre-determined parameters, we would like to very briefly touch upon the published causes of project failure. What we mean by published are the well-known causes that everyone talks about or writes about in project management articles, books, studies, and reports.

From the Standish Group report, there were listed two sets of factors: one set of factors "challenged" the projects and the other set of factors "impaired" the projects. There were 10 factors in each of these sets, and each of these factors was ranked. These factors map well to the 10 knowledge areas of the Project Management Book of Knowledge (PMBoK).

These published causes of project failure may be what you are familiar with at your organization. You then reach deeper into the 10 knowledge areas, and the 47 processes associated with these areas, to find out which process is broken.

We think that knowledge is not an issue. Most professionals already know or can easily find out all the 47 processes listed in the 10 knowledge areas of the PMBoK. It is not about knowing the processes, but more about doing. Doing it right.

When it comes to doing, the doing is done at the individual level. At the individual level, there is rampant disengagement as we have illustrated earlier. Because of that, there is a lot of crisis management that happens day in day out. That is where the root cause is.

We can take each of the factors listed in the Standish report and map it to a task or a set of tasks that were missed, that were not defined, that were not clarified, that were not estimated, that were not tracked, that were not measured, that were not assigned to the right person, and in a nutshell, that were not done right.

That to us is the root cause. To explain further, we will take the analogy of a building.

The Building Analogy

Let's say you visit a building site where a new building is being constructed. You start walking towards this building and from a distance; you count around 20 workers working on it. As you walk closer, you notice a few strange things. You note these down:

- 2 workers are reading a newspaper (Checked out workers).
- 3 workers are building sandcastles (Doing busy work unrelated to project).
- 4 workers are carrying 4 bricks on a plank very slowly (Group task taking longer).
- 5 workers are looking at a big boulder and scratching their heads as to what to do with it. (Task not broken down).
- 4 workers are fixing a wall that had crumbled down (Urgent and important tasks).
- 2 workers are laying out the bricks in order on a wall (right tasks at the right time).

Even if you are not the project manager of this building site, you would still know how to fix some of these issues quickly and easily to get the building constructed right. That is because, with thousands of years of experience in building buildings, even a layman knows a few things about construction. With knowledge work arena being new, this is not the case. (More on knowledge work later)

We think that the core principles of building a structure can be applied to knowledge work. If the foundation is stronger, then the building gets a better chance of not collapsing under its own weight. If we look at projects with this analogy, then at the foundational level there are tasks. Let's imagine these as the building blocks. If we make these building blocks right and stack them up right and line them up right, then there is a good chance that the foundation is taken care of. With a strong foundation, you get a good chance for any structure to be raised up. That is why we have written this book to give a solid grounding on how to implement a system where every task that is worked on is done right. And where the right task is worked on by the right person, and that right task that is worked on by this right person is worked on at the right time, every time.

Trusted System Introduction

The root cause for most project failure, based on our experience and research, is that tasks are not done right. Everyone knows "what" should be done, but still, the "what" does not seem to get done. Brian Robertson in his book *Holacracy: The New Management System for a Rapidly Changing World*, aptly said:

> "people have lots of ideas about what "we" should do … but "we" doesn't do it"

We don't do tasks. The team doesn't do tasks. The individual team member does the task. If everyone on the team does his/her task right, then all the tasks get done right, and the project has great chances of succeeding. Why does that not happen?

The simple answer is that there is no trusted system. There is no trusted system because most systems are copied. This has been aptly explained by Peter Senge in his book *The Fifth Discipline: The Art & Practice of The Learning Organization*. Here is an excerpt from his book.

> "I believe benchmarking best practices can open people's eyes as to what is possible, but it can also do more harm than good, leading to piecemeal copying and playing catch-up. As one seasoned Toyota manager commented after hosting over a hundred tours for visiting executives, "They always say 'Oh yes, you have a Kan-Ban system, we do also. You have quality circles, we do also. Your people fill out standard work descriptions, ours do also.' They all see the parts and have copied the parts. What they do not see is the way all the parts work together." I do not believe great organizations have ever been built by trying to emulate another, any more than individual greatness is achieved by trying to copy another "great person."

In this book, we overcame this problem of parts being copied by taking a holistic approach by building a structure for a trusted system.

When you have a trusted system, you and your team's Mondays or any other workdays will be very different. Here is how it will look. Imagine your desk has many papers strewn all over it.

Each of these papers is a task to do. Anyone looking at this many tasks would be fazed. But you are not. You close your eyes, hold out your hand and turn your palm upward. One paper floats up in the air and slowly lands on your hand. Just like magic. On this paper is the one and only task that you should do. It is the most important task for now... for this moment... for this time.

Not only you, but also each of your team members will be in the same situation. No one can get stuck or be overwhelmed as long as the trusted system AUTOMAGICALLY shows the right tasks to be worked on. The right tasks that will move the project forward!

Who Will Benefit From This Book

The audience for this book is primarily project managers and managers because the focus is for teams to complete their tasks right so that projects are delivered in less than 50% of time. Since the main responsibility of project delivery is with the project managers in matrix organizations and the managers in non-matrix organizations, the primary audience for this book is the project managers and managers who want to deliver projects in less time.

Many of the processes and the tools discussed in this book will help any project cut its time in half, and so can be helpful to even individuals working on their personal or business projects. There are many productivity improvements mentioned in this

MANAGE. LEAD. TRANSFORM.

book that can be helpful for anyone wanting to finish projects more quickly.

In a nutshell, this book will be useful for anyone who is doing a project, managing a project, or paying for a project.

CHAPTER 2

DEFINING STRUCTURE

"Today the network of relationships linking the human race to itself and to the rest of the biosphere is so complex that all aspects affect all others to an extraordinary degree. Someone should be studying the whole system, however crudely that has to be done, because no gluing together of partial studies of a complex nonlinear system can give a good idea of the behavior of the whole."

– Murray Gell-Mann

Knowledge is not an issue. The processes and the actions that need to be done are known. The list of activities and the outputs from these activities are all known. But even then there are schedule overruns on most projects. The average delays in projects are as much as 222%, according to the Standish group report. If you were to go back and do a thorough analysis of how you could have shortened the time frame, then you realize that the project could have been done much earlier. It is a different matter altogether as to why going back and doing lessons learned seems to be a waste of time and so this exercise is not done most of the time. Even if it is done, it is done only to make everyone look good. You know, success has many fathers, but failure is an orphan.

The goal of this book is to shorten the time it takes to complete a project. For that reason, the focus is on simplifying task management since tasks are the building blocks on which all schedules are built. By simplifying task management, we would like the actual doer of the task to become proficient in all aspects of task management. When the doer of the tasks becomes proficient at managing every aspect of a task from estimating, doing, tracking, and measuring, then a new organizational competency is built.

To build this organizational competency, you will structure your existing processes in such a way that this competency is built. In other words you will be arranging your processes. So, the word "Structure" is being used in this book as a verb and not a noun. We will lay out processes for every aspect of the task, and you will structure these processes to best suit your business needs and/or project needs. By using the word structure as a verb we would like to take away the connotation of the noun where structure seems to give a meaning of rigidity. Depending on the projects that you are working on, you can structure the processes to create a trusted system for managing tasks.

Getting the building blocks right is our mantra. With task management as an organizational competency, any organization small or big can leverage the expertise, the time, and the effort of every team member, and align it to bring the most desirable outcomes to fruition for the benefit of the organization.

With this goal in mind, this book is low on theory and high on practical steps. You will not find the definition of what a project is, nor any concepts like earned value management explained here. The reason being, that there are many processes that precede the advanced level of earned value management that don't get implemented. Our focus is to get those processes streamlined first. Also, we want a larger audience that is not necessarily familiar with every aspect of project management to benefit from the structure provided in this book. This structure will provide a set of core principles that can be applied to everyday tasks. Along with these core principles will be a toolset of process steps that can be used to get work done in the right time.

The Current State

Our underlying assumption is that at your company the current state of project delivery success trend has flatlined, or is even moving in a negative direction. With project failure so common, and schedule delays much more common among small, medium, and large companies, we think that your company also has the same problem, and that is the reason you picked our book. You may have tried many newer methodologies like Kanban, Agile, Prince 2, and Scrum. You may even have gone back and forth between Agile and Waterfall. You may have implemented new tools and may have gone back and forth between these tools. It seems like you may be stuck.

Your situation, at best, could be at a standstill, with no improvement in project delivery success year on year. At worst, your situation could be going in the reverse direction, where more projects are failing year after year. More than 40% of CIOs surveyed by Standish Group have mentioned that the failure rate of projects seems to have increased from previous years.

As you start implementing the processes one by one, you will start moving in the right direction. Your company's project delivery success will be a crawl, and then a walk, and then a run as we progress along. In other words, at the end of each of these parts, your speed will increase. With the increase of speed, the delivery time of the projects will decrease, providing you the benefit of more work done in less time.

Needless to say, as more and more work is done in less and less time, the projects can be delivered in less than 50% of the time. Since our approach is holistic, where the processes are fine-tuned to increase the engagement of the employees, the benefits are sustainable for the long-term. It is not a one-time deal by putting all hands on deck to move the needle. It is also not a wait-till-the-end-to-benefit approach. The benefits realization will start happening with each process. Sometimes the process can be implemented in a day of training, and sometimes in a week. So, the benefits are immediate and long lasting.

We understand that this is a big promise. So, let's get you started.

The "Manage" Stage

The first stage "Manage" starts at the ground level to empower the doer of the task. In this part, the processes and tools are laid out so as to build the ground game – the ground game is where the tasks are actually done. The idea is to start moving in the right direction right away. The doer of the task is empowered so that the benefits of the processes are realized in quick time. In other words, the aim is to improve individual productivity in the knowledge work area. Therefore, the first order of business is to understand the nature of knowledge work so as to know the challenges of this work.

Most work in today's day and age is knowledge work.

There are multiple definitions of knowledge work and here are some.

> Business Dictionary Definition
>
> Job, process or task that is distinguished by its specific information content or requirements

Wikipedia Definition

Knowledge work can be differentiated from other forms of work by its emphasis on "non-routine" problem-solving that requires a combination of convergent, divergent and creative thinking.

We would like to provide our own definition so as to simplify knowledge work.

Our Definition

Knowledge work is the work that you do on your device (smartphone, tablet, or computer) even if that work is through e-mail, internet, or mobile apps.

Understanding that most work nowadays is knowledge work, will help in knowing the challenges of knowledge work. The non-routineness of knowledge work causes many major challenges. We will take each of these challenges and provide a solution for them, to empower the doer of the task as well as to help the doer finish his or her individual tasks in the shortest possible time, with great quality.

The "Lead" Stage

Once the individual doers have implemented the processes in the Manage stage and the tasks are getting done more quickly than before, the next stage is to implement processes for the leader of a team to cultivate high performing teams. The word "cultivate" is used deliberately to conjure up images of all the activities that a farmer does, such as, tilling the soil, nurturing the soil, planting seeds, watering the plants, removing the weeds, etc.

Just like a farmer painstakingly cultivates a garden, similarly, the leader of the team; whether the title of the leader is "manager" or "project manager" or "program manager"; needs to cultivate a high performing team. Before we talk about the required characteristics of the leader, let us understand the difference a high performing team makes in comparison to a low performing team.

High Performing Team	Low Performing Team
High Morale	Low Morale
Most risks are identified early because team members take ownership and are proactive.	Critical Risks are not identified because team members are disengaged.
Risks rarely turn into issues	Most risks turn into issues
Big issues look small	Small issues look big
Many tasks are done earlier than estimated	Most tasks are done later than expected
Most outcomes are positive	Most outcomes are negative

As shown above, a high performing team makes a huge difference in terms of getting the work done. The major attributes of a high performing team are as follows:

- Identify as many risks as early as possible
- Proactively work on the risks so that these risks do not become issues
- When faced with big challenges, a high performing team comes together to solve the issues
- Keep high morale, so when tough things happen, solutions are thought out instead of finger pointing

Just like a garden does not grow on its own, a high performing team also needs to be cultivated by the leader of the team. The characteristics needed, at a minimum, by the leader are as follows:

- Calm under pressure.
- Organized.
- Positive.

The processes for transforming any team into a high performing team are laid out in this part of the book. At the end of this stage, the tasks are not only getting done faster, but also the roadblocks for getting the tasks done are being removed.

The "Transform" Stage

A broken process at the top of the food chain will cause major structural issues at every level of the organization. In this part of the book, processes are laid out at the organizational level. The processes at this level are to establish a rallying cry for the organization from which goals for the entire organization are cascaded out timely to all the departments so that every project that each department does can be aligned with the goals of the organization, and in turn, with the rallying cry.

A scene in the movie, "Finding Nemo" will help to imagine the power of alignment toward a single goal. In the final scenes of the movie *Finding Nemo*, Nemo, the little fish and hundreds of other fish are caught in a big fishing net. The fish when caught in the net start swimming in all directions. Nemo rallies these hundreds of fish to swim in one direction, which is toward the bottom of the sea. As more and more fish start swimming in the right direction, the fishing net cannot take combined weight of the fish and falls to the bottom of the sea coming loose, thus releasing all the fish.

This is a great illustration of how, by lining up every effort in the right direction, one can get out of major trouble. In our case, the major trouble is the bleeding caused by failed or delayed projects.

Imagine the success of an organization if every task, even at the lowest level of the organization, is aligned with the topmost goal of the company. Imagine if every effort is aligned in the right direction to move the company forward. Imagine if everyone in the organization rallies behind a single goal, not just once, but every time there is a need. Imagine if there is a trusted system that magically aligns every task to the top most goals of the company. When this happens, the organization as a whole is poised to run by breaking the shackles of disengagement, burnout, and crisis management.

The Structure of the Trusted System

In the upcoming chapters, we will take one process to implement per chapter. We will start out by explaining the situation caused by not having a process, and then we will lay out the steps for implementing the process. Each process stands on three legs; a mindset change, a task to perform, and a measurement. Not following one of the steps will result in losing the benefit of that process.

Starting with the processes for the individual to get the tasks done faster to the processes for the teams to perform at a high level and then processes for the organizations to align, the structure can be given for any organization to deliver meaningful projects in the quickest time possible. In some cases, this time can be reduced by over 50%.

PART 1: MANAGE

"Being busy does not always mean real work. The object of all work is production or accomplishment and to either of these ends there must be forethought, system, planning, intelligence, and honest purpose, as well as perspiration. Seeming to do is not doing."

– Thomas A Edison

CHAPTER 3

OWN YOUR TASKS

"The greatest heroes are those who do their duty in the daily grind of domestic affairs whilst the world whirls as a maddening dreidel."

– Florence Nightingale

The Situation; Hard Work Syndrome

It is a common feeling that most work is assigned and not chosen. This feeling causes what we call "the hard work syndrome." The symptoms of the hard work syndrome are being overwhelmed, loss of focus, and procrastination. Let's unpack this further.

There is a huge difference between what hard work was in olden days to what hard work now is. In olden days, hard work was easily distinguishable in activities like farming, mining, manufacturing, etc. In the Colorado Museum, a mining cave was recreated with the elevator, rock walls with water dripping, and the darkness in the mines. There was also a video presentation of how mining was done. That experience was an eye-opener for us. That was real hard work. It took hours to drill one hole in a wall, this was before dynamite was invented. Tough conditions and real hard work! Today's knowledge work pales in comparison to the hard work that millions of people in olden days had to do when farming, mining, and manufacturing.

In today's world, hard work could be calling an irate customer, doing performance evaluations, making a decision, etc. Tasks that may seem simple but somehow get put on the back burner because we feel that it is hard work. We would like to do *n* number of things before doing these tasks because we feel they are hard. Some of you may be saying to yourselves, "I don't feel like it is hard work to do performance evaluations." Exactly our point! What is hard work to someone else, may not be hard work for you. The task is not stamped as hard work. It is just a task, which based on the employee's temperament, which sometimes the employee may not even know is considered hard work.

The first symptom of this syndrome is being overwhelmed. Whatever task no matter how small or big that comes your way overwhelms you then you have the hard work syndrome.

The second symptom is loss of focus. When you cannot spend more than a few minutes on the task before stepping away or moving onto some other task not because something showed up but just because you want to get away from your task then you have hard work syndrome.

The third symptom is procrastination. When you spend more time thinking about what happens if you don't do the task now, then you have the hard work syndrome.

Process For Taking Ownership of Tasks

Mindset: You have a choice

The first step in the process of taking ownership of tasks is a new mindset. The new mindset is to understand that you are in control. You are in control of your time and your work. You have to understand that you have a choice. The choice is that this is a world of doing. We are on this earth for doing and not for sitting idle. Doing is part of our DNA. Humankind has accomplished a lot so far because of the sheer power of doing something; doing something for the sake of doing.

The mindset change is the most critical aspect of bringing about taking ownership of the tasks. Making the conscious decision that you have chosen to do the task because you have taken the job that you applied for. No one has forced you to take the job.

In the movie, *Devil Wears Prada*, the main protagonist, Andy Sachs, played by Anne Hathaway, is reminded all the time that millions of girls would kill for her job. Whenever someone says that to her, Andy rolls her eyes as though she does not understand why anyone would kill to have her job. A job where all she gets is condescension and zero recognition for her work as a secretary to a bad boss, Miranda Priestly, played so well by Meryl Streep.

In one of the scenes between Andy and her co-worker Nigel, Andy starts complaining that her work is not acknowledged and that her boss does not even say thank you to her. Nigel gives Andy amazing piece of advice. Nigel says, *"Because this place, where so many people would die to work you only deign to work. And you want to know why she doesn't kiss you on the forehead and give you a gold star on your homework at the end of the day. Wake up, sweetheart."*

Trust us when we say that there will be literally a million people who would love to be in your situation if they had a chance. This example was provided to give a context around perception. Around the perception that hard work is not really hard work if you make up your mind that you are not the victim, that you have chosen this work and that you can leave this job whenever you want to find the work that satisfies you.

Task: Find Meaning

The second process step is to find meaning for your tasks. Take your tasks one by one and draw a line of sight from the task to the project to the goals of the company. Even if the goals of the company are not explicitly stated or confusing, you can categorize any goals or projects to either save the company money or make money for the company. Most likely all projects can fall into either one of this category.

At times this can feel like too much of work but continue with it and see if you can find the meaning for your tasks by drawing a line of sight from your lowest level of task to your company's highest goal of either making or saving money.

Measurement: Know the value of tasks

The third process step is to measure. Measure which of your tasks has more bang for the buck; which task is of high value and which is of low value. By high value, we mean if there are multiple projects that you are working on and if one project makes more money for the company versus the other, then the one making more money is of high-value.

Action Steps

- Change your mindset to feel you have a choice. The choice of working on the tasks that have been assigned because you have applied for the job. No one forced you into this job.
- Find meaning by drawing a line of sight from the lowest level of your tasks to the highest mission/goal for your company.
- Measure your high-value tasks to know which tasks give the most bang for the buck.

Results to Be Expected

When you are choosing meaningful and high-value work, then you own the work. Once you own your work, then it should not feel like hard work anymore. The symptoms of being overwhelmed, loss of focus, and procrastination will decrease to a large extent.

The process for taking ownership of tasks is a stand-alone process. You can get this started without any other process. The time to implement this process could be a day or less than a day.

This process can be part of an on-boarding process for a new project or a new team member.

The benefit from this process is immediate. This will definitely improve the engagement level, which in turn, will improve the chances of work getting done on time.

CHAPTER 4

KNOW A TASK FROM A PROJECT

"There's a great satisfaction in knowing that we've made good use of our days, that we've lived up to our expectations of ourselves."

– Gretchen Rubin

The Situation: Project Hidden as a Task

In the current context, we mean the next action step when we say task. Task in this context, is the lowest level of work that cannot be further broken down. Without knowing the lowest level of task, the task cannot be done. To explain this further we need to give an example that has been taken from David Allen, the productivity guru, and the author of the book *Getting*

Things Done: The Art of Stress Free Productivity. We have embellished this example to suit our needs.

Let's say the oil change light comes on in your car. You are very proactive, and immediately add a task in your task management solution that says, "Change oil in the car." Let's add some complexity to this situation. You have moved to a new town. Your car needs a special type of oil only a few trusted oil-service shops carry. Last time you did an oil change through an unknown car servicing shop, your car gave you major trouble. Also, you are cost conscious, and so do not want to pay more than what you have paid before.

The complexity of this situation makes you put some thought into the next steps. You remember your spouse knows someone who has a similar car. Maybe this person will know some trusted oil-service shops. You then have to call one or more of these shops to find out if they carry this special oil, compare prices, and then schedule an oil change. Now, you realize that your task is not one simple task but a series of tasks.

According to David Allen, any work that needs more than one action step to complete should be called a project and per his Getting Things Done (GTD) methodology, this project may not move forward if the immediate action step is not clarified, noted, prioritized, and scheduled. What you thought of a task is now a project according to one of the greatest productivity gurus of this century. You cannot do a project; you can only do action steps or tasks. If you kept the task, "Change Oil in the car" as is, instead of noting down the actual steps you need to do, then most likely, you will put off completing the work of changing oil until a day comes when your car stops in the middle of the road.

Now the task of changing the oil in the car has turned into a crisis - like the most urgent and the most important task.

Process for Knowing a Task from a Project

Mindset: Decide to spend time upfront

When you think of a task and note it down, do you take the time to form a full sentence or just write anything? If you are busy, then it is understandable to make a quick note of anything that can remind you of the task so as not to forget it. But once you have made a note, do you clarify it or leave it at that? If you do not clarify then you need to understand that there could be a project hidden in that note. A note that says "Mom's birthday" is not enough because it could mean "Call mom to wish her birthday" which is a simple task or "Plan Mom's birthday" which is a project.

Making a little effort upfront goes a long way in getting the task done on time. So, the mindset change that needs be made is to spend that additional time needed to clarify a task to know if it is a one-step task or a multi-step project.

Task: Always start with an action verb

The task name has to have an action verb in the present tense at the beginning of the task. A task that says "Pizza" or "Server" or "Module 1.1.5" may seem meaningful when you are writing the task down but somehow hinders the task getting done. Compare that to any task with an action verb in the beginning like "Order Pizza," "Deliver Pizza" or "Eat Pizza." In our experience, we have seen that naming the task with an action verb in the present tense, increases the chances of the task getting done. It may seem like common sense, but we have seen so many tasks during our project audits that did not start with action verbs. It is much needed.

So, the task to perform as part of this process to review all the tasks is that you have to see if any of these tasks do not start with an action verb. If any of these tasks does not have an action verb in front of it, then you need to rename each of these tasks starting with an action verb in the present tense.

Measurement: Quick time estimate

When every task that is assigned to you starts with an action verb in the present tense, you will get an idea whether the task is a 5-minute task or it is a project that will take you days to complete.

Many tasks are left undone when the task takes longer than you estimated. Here, we are not talking about even 3-point estimates. We want you to get a general idea whether the task is a 5-minute effort or an hour or a day or more. We want to make sure that you draw a distinction between tasks that can be done as stand-alone versus tasks hidden as projects.

Action Steps

Here is a summary of action steps for this process.

- Change your mindset to understand that it is way better to spend a little bit more effort upfront to know a task from a project.
- Review all your tasks to make sure every task begins with an action verb in the present tense
- Estimate at a high level to know the approximate time it will take to do the tasks with the focus of understanding that there is no project hidden in the task.

Results to Be Expected

We hope that the distinction between project and task is clear. We do not mean to say that every task that has sub-tasks in the project management world should be called a project. For large size projects, we understand that there will be projects, sub-projects, phases, activities, tasks, sub-tasks, sub-sub-tasks, etc. But, the main point is that you do not immediately know the right task to work on if you cannot differentiate a project from a task.

That is one of the reasons that the task gets on the back burner because enough mental effort is not expended upfront, and then an action verb in a present tense is not used to begin the name of the task, which finally, does not give an idea in what time the task can be done. David Allen aptly said:

> "You don't actually do a project; you can only do action steps related to it. When enough of the right action steps have been taken, some situation will have been created that matches your initial picture of the outcome closely enough that you can call it "done."

No matter how many times you look at a task hidden as a project, the task does not get done because you have not thought of the immediate task and noted it down. In other words, the task will get delayed until your car stops in the middle of the road and you are forced to drop everything that you were doing to manage this crisis. As explained earlier, this example seems very contrived because we do not see cars stopping in the middle of the road for not changing the oil. However, the point that we want to make is that knowing the effort in front of you, helps you in finishing that task.

Once you understand that there is a project hidden in a task, then you need the following process to break down the task.

CHAPTER 5

BREAK DOWN YOUR TASKS

"Nothing is particularly hard if you divide it into small jobs."

– Henry Ford

Situation: Task is too High-level

In our project audits, we come across tasks that do not have the proper level of detail. Usually, the detail is too high-level, but in rare cases the detail is too low-level. This is very rare. There are 5, 10, or 15-minute tasks given out by the team members, and this is not such a bad thing at all. We will talk later about how to take advantage of this low-level breakdown to get the work done on time. The main problem with very high-level tasks, is that it is difficult to know where the task is. What the percentage completion is, and whether that percentage, if known, is accurate.

One program that we audited took the cake in terms of having many high-level tasks. This was a large program with 9 projects in it and was halfway completed when we were asked to audit it. As part of our audit, we went through the project schedules of all the projects. Different vendors were doing most of the work on this program. But this work was plugged as one task per vendor in the projects.

Even though there were detailed tasks that the team were doing, the vendor tasks were one-line items. There was a single line item in MS project that showed one task by one of the vendors for 17 folks for the duration of 3 months. Imagine it! 17 full-time resources charging day-by-day, week-by-week their 40 hours to one line item. When we asked for the breakdown of this task, there was no breakdown given to us because the vendor did not have one. It was unbelievable. There was no way the vendor could give the percentage complete on this task accurately to the program every week without a breakdown of the tasks.

Knowing the amount of time spent on a task does not mean the task is completed by that amount in percentage terms. This logic was lost on the vendors, and after much negotiation and many planning sessions we were able to break down these high-level tasks into detailed lower level tasks.

Process for Breaking Down High-level Tasks

Mindset: Understand that "we" doesn't do it.

There cannot be more than one person on a single task. You have to have your task separated out from the group task. Unless it is a meeting, there is no group task in the arena of knowledge work that is done by two or more people at the same time. So, when you have tasks that have more than one person assigned, you need to separate your task. You need to have a task that has only you as the resource on it. It is critical for implementing this process.

The mindset change for implementing this process is to understand that "we" doesn't do it.

Task: Break down the high-level task

There are many ways how you can go about breaking down a high-level task. For example, if the task is to paint a house, and let's say there are four people working on painting the house, then the task has to split in such a way that each person has his own unique task. In this instance, there can be multiple tasks like, "paint living room," "paint dining room," etc. Even after breaking down this task, if there is more than one person going to work on the task, "paint living room," then this task can further be split into "paint living room – north wall," "paint living room – south wall," etc. Let's say the north wall is a long wall, and two people need to work on it. Then the task can be split into two tasks assigned to each person that should say,

"Paint north wall – left side," "Paint north wall – right side." The tasks have to be split to show each person assigned to the sub-task.

Let's say the task cannot be broken down in meaningful bites. It is one big task and does not have any meaningful sub-tasks. Let's say there are two people assigned to this "Do Big Task." You need to split this task into two tasks as shown below.

"Do Big Task by Person A"
"Do Big Task by Person B"

Measurement: Find out a base unit for a task

After breaking down a high-level task assigned to one person, there could still be a large task that can span multiple hours, days or weeks. A large task may mean different things to different folks. So, you need to come up with a unit of work that can be customized for you. The unit of work could be the amount of time you take to work on a task and then take a break of at least 15 minutes. After this break, you may come back to do the same task or start another one.

With this rule of thumb, depending on your work style and the type of work, the unit of work could be 10 hours or 1 hours or 15 minutes. For example, if you are a workaholic or love the work, then you may work on that task for 10 hours straight without taking a break of more than 15 minutes in between. There are many times when folks eat lunch at their desks while working and take very quick breaks to get back to work. If your work is demanding like that, then 4 to 10 hours could be a good unit of work. If the work is intense and drains you in less than an hour and you cannot pick that work until the next day, then 15 minutes to 1 hour could be a good unit of work in this case.

Now that you have determined your unit of work, any task that needs more than one unit of work needs to be broken down. Many times it is not possible to break down the task and have a meaningful name for the sub-task. The best way to do that is to name the task as follows:

Big Task – Unit 1
Big Task – Unit 2
Big Task – Unit n

This breakdown is useful in many ways, and we will go over that in detail later in this chapter.

Action Steps

Here is the summary of action steps needed to implement the process for breaking down tasks by person and by measurable unit.

- Mindset change is to understand that "we" doesn't do it when it comes to tasks, and so you need to make sure that high-level tasks are broken down in such a way that there is one task per person.

- Tasks that need to be performed to implement this process is to figure out a creative way, if needed, to break down a task and name it accordingly.
- Measure the unit of task for your situation so that a large task can be broken down meaningfully.

Results to Be Expected

Some of the project management systems may not have the capacity to have detailed tasks broken down to one-person one base unit tasks. If that is the case, then a supplemental task management system has to be added to track these tasks. There are multiple task management systems available that can seamlessly take as many tasks as needed without causing performance degradation or an admin nightmare.

Despite the effort that can sometimes go into breaking down the tasks, the benefits are many. We will give one example here for the biggest benefit.

For instance, let's say you have a "Big Task" that will take 4 weeks to complete. Let's say your base unit of a task is a week. You have now broken down the Big Task into 4 tasks Big Task - week 1, Big Task week 2... etc. If, in the first week, you were not able to spend enough time on the task and you need another week to complete it, then in the first week you know that the task is going to be delayed by a week. You can then take some measures to get the task back on track. If the task has not been broken down, then you may only discover the task delay at the end of the fourth week when it is too late to make any adjustments.

The earlier you get the warning signal of a task delay; the better off you will be in adjusting the subsequent tasks.

CHAPTER 6

AVOID MULTITASKING

"People think focus means saying yes to the thing that you've got to focus on. But that's not what it means at all. It means saying no to the hundred other good ideas that there are."

– Steve Jobs

Situation: Multitasking Troubles

It is now a well-known fact that our brains do not have the capacity to multitask. Our brains can focus on only one task at a time. This is a vast subject with a great amount of research that has been done. Laws have been passed to stop multitasking while driving. Cell phone usage while driving or texting while driving will get you into trouble with the traffic cops. Even then, multitasking happens on the roads. At work it is even more prevalent. Suffice it to say that it is a norm rather than the exception.

The well-known and well-documented effect of multitasking is the loss of productivity. As many as 2.3 hours of a typical 8-hour work day are lost to multitasking. The lesser-known effects of multitasking are the misinterpretations and miscommunications that happen at the workplace. The most common way of multitasking is reading emails or instant messaging while in meetings. During this type of multitasking, the smallest issue is someone getting distracted and asking the speaker to repeat the question. This is the smallest issue. The biggest issue is when decisions are made that are not properly understood because someone was multitasking. To illustrate this, here is a made-up story of a project manager failing at a simple task due to multitasking.

The Story

Once upon a time, there was a project manager who wanted to take his team to Disney World in Orlando for a JAD session. Since his team is virtual, he schedules a teleconference call for the next week. The subject of the meeting is sent as "JAD session in Disney World, Orlando- let's decide on the date."

A day before the meeting, he sends out an agenda with the possible dates and the logistics for the JAD session.

The team is comprised of 10 people, and everyone attends the meeting. After the role call, the project manager states the purpose of the conference call as a brainstorming session to decide on the date for the JAD session in Disney World, Orlando.

Studies have revealed that only 1 in 10 people read an agenda. So, the news is a surprise for 9 of the team members. 2 of these team members have multiple concerns with either the idea of travel or the choice of destination. So, they immediately start instant messaging their team members. Instant Messages start flying around which go on the lines of...

"Where is the budget for the travel?"
"Who will take care of my fish?"
"Why Orlando?"

4 out of 10 team members are lost to multitasking, thanks to Instant Messenger, while the project manager is discussing the reasons, logistics, and purpose of this meeting,

2 other team members open up their browsers and start checking out the fun activities that you can do in Orlando.

2 team members receive an email notification that distracts them, and they get disengaged from the meeting.

So, all in all, 8 out of 10 multitask and fail to follow the ensuing discussion. Only 2 participate and the decisions are made about the date, logistics, etc. After the meeting, the PM receives many questions from the multitasking team members regarding the logistics, the date, and the reasoning behind the venue, along with the purpose. Since all of these items were part of the agenda and were discussed by the PM and 2 of the 10 engaged team members, the PM gets confused. The PM thinks that he is not doing a good job at communicating. Since 90% of a PM's job is communications, according to many PMI articles (we don't agree with this but that's a different story), the PM gets frustrated and cancels the JAD session.

So, the PM fails at a very simple task.

We understand that the example is very contrived, and most of the time, the consequences are not that severe. But the point that we would like to make is that there are some problems that are caused by multitasking which are misinterpreted as communication problems. Understanding the potential disruption that multitasking can cause is the first step in avoiding multitasking.

Process to avoid multitasking

Mindset: Multitasking makes you stupid

With various studies, the myth of multitasking has been busted. In the arena of knowledge work, your mind can only work on one task at a time. It is also the most effective way of doing things. Therefore, here is an excerpt from a best-selling book *Brain Rules: 12 Principles for surviving and Thriving at Work, Home, and School* written by Dr. John P Medina, who is a developmental molecular biologist. There are many examples that John Medina has given in his book regarding the ineffectiveness of multitasking. Here is one such excerpt.

> "Three researchers at Stanford University noticed the same thing about the undergraduates they were teaching, and they decided to study it. First, they noticed that while all the students seemed to use digital devices incessantly, not all students did. True to stereotype, some kids were zombified, hyperdigital users. But some kids used their devices in a low-key fashion: not all the time, and not with two dozen windows open simultaneously. The researchers called the first category of students Heavy Media Multitaskers. Their less frantic colleagues were called Light Media Multitaskers. If you asked heavy users to concentrate on a problem while simultaneously giving them lots of distractions, the researchers wondered, how good was their ability to maintain focus? The hypothesis: Compared to light users, the heavy users would be faster and more accurate at switching from one task to another, because they were already so used to switching between browser windows and projects and media inputs. The hypothesis was wrong. In every attentional test the researchers threw at these students, the heavy users did consistently worse than the light users. Sometimes

dramatically worse. They weren't as good at filtering out irrelevant information. They couldn't organize their memories as well. And they did worse on every task-switching experiment. Psychologist Eyal Ophir, an author of the study, said of the heavy users: "They couldn't help thinking about the task they weren't doing. The high multitaskers are always drawing from all the information in front of them. They can't keep things separate in their minds." This is just the latest illustration of the fact that the brain cannot multitask. Even if you are a Stanford student in the heart of Silicon Valley."

If you are not yet convinced, then please Google multitasking studies, and you will come across many studies. One of these studies has concluded that multitasking lowers IQ levels worse than the usage of marijuana.

Make this mental shift that multitasking is not just counter-productive but also makes you stupid. Someone has aptly said: "Multitasking is the opportunity to screw up more than one thing at a time."

Task: Switch off the device

If it is possible, then the movie rule should be followed in the meetings. The laptop should be closed, and the cell phone should be switched off, or at least, put on silent mode to avoid any distraction. This is a common thing nowadays when the meetings are critical. One other thing that has helped tremendously for our virtual team members is switching off the monitor when you are in a teleconference.

It is a daily occurrence to see meetings derailed because someone was not paying attention. We are sure this could be one of your pet peeves too. There is one real incident that we would like to share here to show how it is a good idea to not read emails while you are leading the meetings.

> "The Program Director was leading a status meeting on a large program, and in this meeting, there were more than 100 people on the teleconference call. While giving the status of the program, the program director stops in the middle of the sentence and starts crying. You can imagine the confusion of the folks on the call. After a minute or two of sobbing, she gathers herself and lets everyone know that she got some bad news in an email. It seems her friends had gone mountain hiking and were missing. She was worried about their whereabouts, and in the middle of this meeting she gets an email notification and inadvertently glances at the email only to find out that her friends were dead. Anyone would have a similar, if not the same reaction as she had."

The point we would like to make with the above example is that if not this big of a distraction, there is going to be some distraction when you glance at your emails while you are in a meeting. It is bound to happen. Avoiding these distractions by taking some serious measures like switching off your device or switching off your monitor or turning off your email notifications will go a long way in focusing on the task at hand.

Measurement: Know your focus time

In one of the episodes of Shark Tank, a TV series where entrepreneurs pitch their companies to a group of investors, an entrepreneur, Maneesh Sethi, presented a revolutionary product that keeps you on task by giving you a small electric shock. It seems that the idea for the product came from a productivity experiment where Sethi hired a girl to slap him whenever he got off task. This productivity experiment is documented on his blog and this experiment lead to this product, Pavlok. The idea is to avoid distraction, and give yourself a shock whenever you get off task. We are not recommending this product, since we have not used it. For us, this sounds extreme and may not work for the same reasons the investors on Shark Tank did not invest in the product.

However, the point we are trying to make is that focusing on a single task for any amount of time is getting difficult. That is why products like these are showing up in the market. What will work in this situation is for you to know your own personal focus time. Having said that, we know that some tasks are easy to focus and work on for a long time and some are not. Either way, you can time yourselves to find out your average focus time.

Start with a timer for 5 minutes. If you fail to stay on task before the timer goes off, then you know your focus time is less than 5 minutes. If you stay on task till the timer goes off, then you can increase the timer every time by 5 minutes to find out your average focus time.

Action Steps

Here is the summary of action steps needed to implement the process to avoid multitasking.

- Mindset change is to understand that multitasking is counter-productive, and can also make you stupid.
- Task that needs to be performed to implement this process is to get in the habit of switching off your devices to focus on the task at hand.
- Measure your average focus time to stay on a task.

Results to Be Expected

One of the benefits of this process is to increase productivity up to 2.3 hours every 8 hours. That is almost 1/3 of time saved on your tasks. Depending on your own personal focus time, you will find out how much improvement can be made in your case. This is a tangible benefit.

The intangibles are the benefits derived by less miscommunication on tasks and projects.

CHAPTER 7

PRIORITIZE YOUR TASKS

"Things which matter most must never be at the mercy of things which matter least."

– Johann Wolfgang von Goethe

Situation: Too many high priorities

When everything is a high priority, then nothing is a priority. It so happens that when there is too much to do, we often get overwhelmed, and instead of working on any one task out of all the pending tasks, we watch TV or surf the Internet. It is the same thing at work too, if there are multiple tasks that need to be worked on, then we get overwhelmed, and tend to spend the entire workday reading and responding to e-mails. There are enough e-mails received in our inboxes to fill an entire workday without getting any tasks done. In this scenario, we are doing busy work that will not show any progress towards something that needs to be accomplished.

When there are too many critical or high priorities, it usually means that not enough effort was put into prioritization. In other words, it is equivalent to zero prioritization. So, when picking up a task to work on, the outcome is the same if there are too many high priorities or zero priorities. The outcome is that whatever task you pick on will not be the right task.

As shown earlier, hard work is different in the context of knowledge work and to avoid hard work, the task that is picked up to work on could be anything but the right task. In this scenario, it will look like tasks are being worked on, e-mails are read and sent, work seems to be happening, but the right task is not getting done.

Process for prioritizing your tasks

Mindset: Only One # 1 Priority

At any point in time, there can be only one #1 Priority. There is no two ways about it. There are many ways to determine the #1 priority. In chapter 3, we showed one way of doing that. You can take an inventory of the tasks and line each of these tasks to the projects and from the projects to the goals of the company. Most goals are ranked, and that is one way to know which tasks is of high value.

If all your tasks are linked to one goal, then you can look at the prioritization of the projects and determine which one project is of a higher priority, which will then determine the priority of your task.

If all your tasks belong to only one project, then you can look at the due date of the tasks to determine the priority based on which task is due soonest. This is a general guideline for determining the priority of the tasks. If you are working on multiple tasks in the day, then the only challenge is that you may have to do the prioritization multiple times during the day.

Initially, this may be a lot of effort. But the majority of the effort will only be for the first time, assuming that your company's goals stay the same for most of the year, and the projects stay the same for most of the month. In this scenario, the initial effort will be more, but then the effort will be reduce each time you prioritize.

Bottom-line, there cannot be two #1 priorities at any point in time.

Task: # 1 Priority need to be done ASAP

Once you make the mental shift that at any point in time you will have only one #1 priority task, then the next thing to do is to complete that task as soon as possible. Let's say you do the above exercise and decide on the #1 priority, and per the schedule given to you this # 1 priority task is not due until 5 PM today. It is now 9:30 AM, and you have estimated that it will take around 2 hours to complete this task. This task needs to be worked on immediately and should be completed in the next two hours or less. That is the power of setting the #1 priority.

A #1 priority task is due right away. It needs to be worked on right away, and needs to be completed immediately. That is the discipline needed for this process to be successful.

Measurement: Know how many priority changes happen

An important measurement here is to see how your priorities change. How many times during the day or week or month are your #1 priority tasks changed after you start working on them? This is a key metric that needs to be known so that you can manage your work.

Action steps

Here is the summary of action steps needed to implement the process to prioritize your tasks.

- Mindset change is to understand that at any point in time, you need to have only one #1 priority task.
- The #1 priority task must be worked on immediately since any #1 Priority task is due right away.
- Measure how many times in a day or a week or a month your #1 priority changes after you have started working on them.

Results to Be Expected

Knowing the #1 priority is very helpful in getting the tasks done on time. The process of going through the list of tasks to decide on the #1 priority will get refined as it is practiced more and more. Having too many high priorities is counter-productive. The discipline of picking up the #1 priority every time you start your day or your week is going to be very helpful in staying focused on the critical task.

CHAPTER 8

SCHEDULE YOUR BUZZ

"With such a vast and wonderful library spread out before us, we often skim books or read just the reviews. We might already have encountered the Greatest Idea, the insight that would have transformed us had we savored it, taken it to heart, and worked it into our lives."

– Jonathan Haidt

Situation: Communications Overload

With the ease of communications, the carbon copying and the group messaging, the communication channels are being overloaded. E-mail is no longer a reliable channel of communication at work because there is no guarantee that your work e-mail will be read, let alone responded to. Because of the bottleneck in this channel of communications, Instant messaging channels are being predominantly used to communicate, even though that is not their purpose.

Now, even those channels have been overloaded to such an extent that a task can get lost in these channels of communications. So, the term "dropping the ball" in knowledge work parlance has ceased to be a bad thing anymore. If there is a ball dropped, then it no longer is the fault of the ball dropper, because who can understand a task from the barrage of communications coming at them. You barely have time to scan the communications. So, people have been using for years: "Action Required" or "John Doe, please respond..." in the subject of the e-mail.

All these communication methods have notifications too. A few years back, the only notifications that you got on your smartphone were e-mail, calendar, or text. Now, every app notifies you. Facebook, WhatsApp, YouTube, Twitter, and many more. In all these notifications, if there is a task notification, then the notification can be easily lost. Another potential dropped ball is if your task comes to you via your smartphone. These never ending stream of notifications also cause you to get easily distracted. It is not uncommon to open your phone to check the time, and spend 15 minutes checking your Facebook feed.

Going through these communications takes time, which is usually not accounted for. To overcome this situation, we suggest that you schedule your buzz; which could be email or instant messaging or Facebook or Twitter.

Process for scheduling your buzz

Mindset: Your buzz takes time

You need to account for the time you spend on your buzz. Your buzz has become an important part of your life. Ignoring the time commitment needed for this buzz is not going to help. It is also not practical to say that this buzz is unnecessary. So, it is better to assume that some, if not most, of this buzz is needed. Also, there is no stopping the progress of technology. Sometimes important work is also being done as part of this buzz. That is why it is a good workable assumption to operate with. Making the shift in your mindset that your buzz is somewhat needed in today's world, and that it takes some considerable chunk of time, is the first step in not getting overwhelmed with the communications overload.

Task: Schedule time on calendar

The best way to handle your buzz is to schedule it. Yes, schedule it on your calendar. Schedule processing of emails; schedule processing of instant messages; schedule processing Facebook feeds; schedule processing of Twitter. Whether you like it or not, the most productive people are already doing that. The most prolific users of twitter are also busy professionals who are getting a lot of things done in their lives. If they can do that, you can too.

The underlying principle in scheduling the buzz is that an enormous amount of time can be wasted if a structured process is not put in place. For example, everyone is overwhelmed with email. A few years back, only managers or top executives had overflowing inboxes. Now, almost everyone, even at the lowest level of an organization has an email problem. There are times when you can spend an entire 8 hours of a workday - reading, re-reading, replying, and re-replying to emails without getting any tasks done.

With this underlying principle, you can approach your buzz as part of your workload. How much of this workload is needed? Is an hour a day good enough or 2 hours or 3 hours? Since the buzz can take more or less time, depending on what's happening in your world, you may want to average out the time needed. Let's say your average is two hours, then you can break down these two hours into four 30-minute events that can be scheduled on your calendar.

Measurement: Know your baseline

When you start scheduling your buzz on your calendar, you do not know exactly how long you need to spend on your buzz. As you start following your schedule, make a note of whether you are able to go through all your communications in the time allocated. Most people underestimate the time it normally takes to process their communications. As you keep following your schedule and monitoring the time it takes to process your communications, you get a very clear idea of how much time you need per day to just go through communications. This is your baseline, and you need to adjust your calendar so as to account for this time.

It is better to not be too aggressive in the first few weeks. Don't try to run a marathon on the very first day when you start running. Similarly, you need to pace yourself so that you are not overwhelmed. Aim for small victories. The buzz may take more than your planned or unplanned time. There are some behaviors that will not go away in the very first week or so. You will still check your buzz when your phone buzzes or when you check your phone for knowing time. It is bound to happen. So, the best way is to plan for the vagaries of the environment.

The above issue of not taking environmental factors into consideration has been beautifully explained in the book, *Triggers: Creating Behavior That Lasts—Becoming the Person You Want to Be,* written by the best-selling author Marshall Goldsmith. Here are a couple of quotes from that book that highlight the common issues with doing the tasks as planned.

> "The willpower we assume when we set a goal rarely measures up to the willpower we display in achieving that goal."

> "If we do not create and control our environment, our environment creates and controls us."

Action steps

Here is the summary of action steps needed to implement the process to schedule your buzz.

- Mindset change is to understand that your buzz takes considerable time.
- Start with a rough estimate, and schedule time for your communications throughout your day by blocking your calendar.
- Measure your baseline time for processing all your communications either on a daily or a weekly basis.

Results from this process

Knowing that you have time scheduled for your communications can take away the temptation to look or glance at your notifications as they come in. It is a good habit to develop. A lot of time can be saved by batch processing your communications. It will also help in avoiding multitasking. A further benefit is it will help to keep you focused at the task at hand.

CHAPTER 9

REPORT YOUR TASKS RIGHT

"You either did or you didn't - there is no try."

– Steve Jobs

Situation: Inaccurate task reporting

The problem with task reporting is three-fold: the accuracy, the timing, and what done means. If only the percentage of task completed is known, then it may not be accurate. Most project managers make this mistake of asking for the percentage complete, when in reality, the answer they get can be so inaccurate depending on whom you ask. For example, if you asked a team member for the percentage complete on a task, and that team member says it is 50% complete, then depending on who the doer of the task is the task could be 0% complete or 50% complete. Let us explain.

If the team member is an IT developer, then the thought process that a developer follows is quite different from that of an IT tester. To a developer, a coding task is 50% complete without even putting pen to paper, in other words, not even writing a single line of code. You may think, how is that possible? This is possible only to a developer, because the developer has thought about this task in the shower or while driving to work and come up with the idea of how to code it. That's it. The difficult part was coming up with the idea how to code it. Now that the difficult part is done, to an IT developer the task is now 50% complete. It is not to say that every developer would do that, but it could be more common than you think.

The second problem is with the timing of the task update. Usually, any issues with a task are discovered after the fact, and the longer it is after the fact, the more it is problematic. If there is a task that gets delayed or is blocked, then the sooner it is known, the better it will be to adjust. Sometimes, the task reporting is set up in such a way that the delayed tasks are not known for more than a week or two. If that is how the task reporting structure is set-up, then you know about a task delay way after the fact. This is a very big problem.

The third problem is with task completion. The problem with task completion is that there can be different sets of understanding as to what "done" means. For example, the task

"Get Pizza" may mean "Order Pizza" to someone or "Get Pizza delivered" or to someone else "Pick-up Pizza." Depending on how the task is understood, it can be a simple task of ordering pizza online or an hour-long task of going to the pizza restaurant and picking up the pizza. So, a clear understanding of what "done" means needs to be communicated to the doer.

Sometimes, task completion is not reported correctly. Saying that the task is 90 - 95 % complete is common. In the project management world, this problem is given a name *"The 90% syndrome,"* where the task is marked as 90% complete but it takes as much time to complete the remaining 10% as it took to get to 90%. The causes for this problem can be varied. It is like driving downtown traversing 9 miles in 10 minutes and taking 10 more minutes to drive the last mile. This happens all the time. But there are times when some folks give the task completion as 90%, so the project manager thinks the task is almost complete and stops bothering the doer of the task. This is common too.

To overcome the issues caused by inaccurate reporting, the following process needs to be implemented.

Process for Accurate Task Reporting

Mindset: Observe the blind pass rule

The mindset change that needs to be made is to observe "the blind pass rule." In basketball, a blind pass, also known as a no-look pass, is done when a player looks in one direction but passes the ball to his teammate in a different direction, causing the defense to be confused. There is a high amount of trust and awareness of the situation when attempting these blind passes. To build similar awareness and trust in the workplace, the blind pass rule equates to where a task is assigned and not followed up. There is energy, effort, and time lost in following-up. Most managers or project managers are "glorified babysitters" when it comes to managing tasks. Sometimes, all they do is follow-up, follow-up, and follow-up.

By understanding the inefficiencies caused by follow-ups, you as the doer of the task should implement the blind pass rule. The blind pass rule states that the doer of the task needs to build trust by communicating the status of any assigned task before it is followed-up. For example, let's say a task is due tomorrow and you just realize that you will not be able to complete that task by tomorrow. You need to immediately communicate the potential delay of the task. The same applies to when the task is going to be done earlier or on time. The responsibility is now shifted on the doer of the task instead of the giver of the task.

Just like in basketball, the doer of the task has to build that trust that when the task is assigned, the doer will receive it and that it is now the doer's responsibility to catch the ball. In other words, it is the failure of the doer to not communicate the task status. If the follow-up is made, then the doer has failed at reporting. Grasping this concept is very important, and so we are going to repeat it.

"If a follow-up is made then the doer has failed at reporting."

Why is that? The reasons can be many. Maybe the person following-up is worried that the task will not be done if not followed up. Maybe the doer of the task has a history of not completing tasks on time. Whatever may be the reasons, it is the failure on the doer's part if the task is followed-up.

How powerful can this be in the real world when the blind pass rule is implemented and fully practiced? The stress on both parties can be eliminated using this rule.

Task: Report right

Whenever you have to report on where you are with the task, you need to provide the full picture as to where you are with the task. Here is an example to show how to report right on the task.

Let's say you are working on a task that has been estimated at 100 hours, and this task will take a month to complete.

In the first week, you work 20 hours on the task. When the project manager gets this information, it will be assumed that the task is 25% complete. Everything seems to be on track from the project manager's perspective. But from your perspective, only you can know whether the remaining task will be done in 80 hours, more or less. Let's say you do not take the time to figure out the remaining hours you need to complete the task. In this scenario, at the end of the month, you will let your project manager know that you may need additional hours. That is too late. You need to provide the remaining hours in the very first report. Is it 80 hours or more or less? Based on this additional information, the accurate status of the task will be known, otherwise, the correct status of the task will be known pretty late, which is not a good thing to have to adjust.

In the above example, we assumed that the base unit of your task is a month. That is a big time period, that should be chunked down into smaller tasks per our process laid out earlier in chapter 5. If you followed that process, then you would have, at a minimum, 4 weekly tasks. Now, we will show the advantage of chunking down the tasks and an innovative way of handling any delay of the tasks.

When the big task has been broken down, the task name of the big task can be, "Do Big Task – Week 1" and the estimate for this task can be 20 hours. At the end of the week, if you have worked 20 hours, then you need to mark this task as complete, calculate the remaining hours to complete the task, and if more than 80, then create one more task, "Do Big Task – Week 5." This will immediately show that the task has been delayed by a week. In the very first week, the project manager will know that the "Do Big Task" task has been delayed by a week.

Reporting the right status of the task from the beginning will help adjust the subsequent tasks.

Measurement: Know the actual time spent on a task

Let's say you are tasked with going from point A to Point B in 30 minutes. In the following scenarios, let's see what time is the right time for the completion of your task.

1. Scenario 1: You get lost on your way and somehow reach Point B in 45 minutes
2. Scenario 2: You hit traffic and reach Point B in 1 hour
3. Scenario 3: Your car breaks down. You get it fixed and finally reach Point B in 3 hours.
4. Scenario 4: You stop for lunch on your way and then reach point B in 2 hours

In none of these scenarios, do you reach the destination in the estimated time. Also, in none of these scenarios, will you know what the right time is to go from point A to point B. Since you never kept track of how long you took a break, how long it took to fix the broken car, how long you were sitting in the traffic, and for how long you were going in circles before you reached Point B, you will not know if you could have reached Point B in 5 minutes or more or less? You don't know the right amount of time that was needed for completing the task.

Not knowing the actual time is not ok because there are not many tasks that you would do only once. There is a likelihood that this task, or a similar task, will be done later if not by you then by someone else. That is why knowing the actual time to complete a task will help a lot for future planning.

Action steps for this process

Here is the summary of action steps needed to implement the process to report your tasks right.

- Mindset change is to understand that a task follow up is a failure on your part.
- Report the tasks correctly by providing additional information of time remaining to complete the task.
- Measure the actual time it takes to complete the task to help in future estimation and planning.

Results to Be Expected

Reporting a task correctly will provide early warning signs of any task delays. The earlier a task delay is known, the more time the project manager will have to adjust the project schedule. It all starts with shifting the mindset to make sure everyone is transparent about where the tasks are at. There should not be follow-ups, since it wastes time as well as good will. To follow-up on a task, a project manager has to remember the due date of a task and then follow-up on time to know where the task is. If this admin task is taken away, then it frees up the time of the project manager to do more value-added activities. The loss of good will and trust is also a factor, since the person being followed-up on may not like the follow-up, which sometimes comes out as nagging.

When the actual time is known on every task, then future estimates of similar tasks can get more accurate.

CHAPTER 10

FROM MANAGING TO LEADING

"Every revolutionary idea seems to evoke three stages of reaction. They may be summed up by the phrases: 1- It's completely impossible. 2- It's possible, but it's not worth doing. 3- I said it was a good idea all along."

– Arthur Clarke

Bottom-up Approach

The processes listed from chapter 3 to chapter 9 help produce immediate benefits of getting the tasks done faster and quicker. Our approach has been a bottom-up one so that the tasks on the projects don't get delayed, but if delayed, then are known right away so the project schedule can be adjusted. If you recall the story of "The Emperor Has No Clothes" the crooked tailors working on the Emperor's clothes are shown as busy cutting some imaginary cloth. When implementing processes and tools, sometimes it feels like there is a lot of busy work happening but no immediate and tangible benefit coming out of it. That is the main reason we started out with the bottom-up approach.

In this bottom-up approach, the processes that we have laid out so far are as follows:

1. Own your tasks
2. Know a task from a project
3. Break down your tasks
4. Avoid Multitasking
5. Prioritize your tasks
6. Schedule your buzz
7. Report your task right

Each of these processes follows a structure of switching to the right mindset, performing a task, and then measuring it to get better at completing tasks on time. So, the bottom-up approach is to empower the doer of the task and shift the responsibility toward the doer. Jim Collins, in his book, *Good to Great: Why Some Companies Make the Leap and Others Don't,* writes about managing systems and not people. Here is a quote from that book.

> "The good-to-great companies built a consistent system with clear constraints, but they also gave people freedom

and responsibility within the framework of that system. They hired self-disciplined people who didn't need to be managed, and then managed the system, not the people."

These 7 processes will greatly help in increasing the engagement of your employees so that they are self-managed. These self-managed employees can usher in "Doerocracy" within your company.

Doerorcacy

We came across the term "doerocracy" and immediately fell in love with it. This term came to our attention in the book, *The Connection Algorithm: Take Risks, Defy the Status Quo, and Live your passions*, written by Jesse Tevelow. It seems that Bart Lorang, the CEO of the company Full Contact, coined this term and here is what he meant by this term.

> "If you want to be a leader, simply DO stuff. Don't ask anyone else's permission. That's what a **Doerocracy** is."

We liked this term a lot and would like to provide our own definition to it.

> **Doerocracy** is the bottom-up approach of implementing processes that empower the doer to own the tasks, define the tasks, prioritize the tasks, report the tasks, and do the tasks at the right time, in the least amount of time, every time.

As explained earlier, there is more disengagement at the individual contributor level in an organization than at any other level. For disengaged workers, most work seems hard work, and so the tasks take longer and get delayed, which in turn, causes projects to be delayed. Doerocracy will turn things around in a short time.

The Manage Stage

In this stage, the benefits realization of implementing all 7 processes will start happening in the first week or two. Depending on the size of the project teams and the existing delays in the projects, this stage will seem slow. Since the goal was to start moving in the right direction, let us illustrate with a sample scenario of an engaged worker identifying a risk and turning a project around.

By avoiding multitasking, your team member listens in with their full attention to an ensuing discussion in your meeting. This team member sees a risk in the approach being discussed, takes ownership of the task, realizes that the task is a project in itself, breaks down the tasks in the project, prioritizes these tasks, schedules these on the calendar, does these tasks and reports them right to you. If the risk was not identified, then you would have come across an issue so late in the project that your project could have been delayed, if not failed. I am sure as a project manager you would have been in this situation multiple times when an issue was found that had no corresponding risk associated with it.

Focus on Execution

A bottom-up approach shifts the focus on execution right away. We will talk about strategy in part 3 of this book but most companies start with strategy, and when it comes to execution, lose steam. Execution is where all the work is, along with all the pain. Execution is where the rubber meets the road. Larry Bossidy, one of the gurus on execution, has some strong words for leaders who don't focus on execution. In his book, *Execution: The Discipline of Getting Things Done,* Larry said:

> "people think of execution as the tactical side of business, something leaders delegate while they focus on the perceived "bigger" issues. This idea is completely wrong. Execution is not just tactics—it is a discipline and a system. It has to be built into a company's strategy, its goals, and its culture. And the leader of the organization must be deeply engaged in it. He cannot delegate its substance. Many business leaders spend vast amounts of time learning and promulgating the latest management techniques. But their failure to understand and practice execution negates the value of almost all they learn and preach. Such leaders are building houses without foundations."

In our opinion, Doerocracy is the discipline and the system that Larry Bossidy is talking about that can help with execution. The idea is that if the doer of the task is empowered, then the task gets done in the best way. If more doers are empowered, then more tasks get done the right way, more projects get delivered the right way, and maybe, the right projects get delivered quickly. When all these things happen, then lo and behold, your organization's strategy gets executed in the right way.

We are jumping the gun here by talking about strategy and will go over strategy in depth when we come to part 3. With the conclusion of the Manage stage, the processes at the lowest level of an organization are implemented and it is time to move to the "Lead" stage where the processes at the team level can be implemented.

PART 2: LEAD

"Individual commitment to a group effort--that is what makes a team work, a company work, a society work, a civilization work."

--Vince Lombardi

CHAPTER 11

LEAD RIGHT

"People grant you power because they expect you to provide them with a service. If you lose yourself in relishing the acclaim and power people give you, rather than on providing the services people will need to restore their adaptability, ultimately you jeopardize your own source of authority."

– Heifetz, Ronald A.; Linsky, Marty

Situation: The Micromanager

In chapter 1, we have shown that disengagement is common and prevalent. We then talked about its impact on projects. But on purpose, we did not go into its causes. There are two reasons why we did not discuss these causes. The first reason is that there are no processes that need to be implemented at the doer level to address the causes of disengagement. The second reason is that a top-down process to eliminate disengagement is going to backfire if the leadership is the primary cause of it. Gary Hamel, beautifully illustrates this point in his book, "Future of Management."

> "The real damper on employee engagement is the soggy, cold blanket of centralized authority. In most companies, power cascades downwards from the CEO.
>
> Not only are employees disenfranchised from most policy decisions, they lack even the power to rebel against egocentric and tyrannical supervisors."

In the same vein, the 7 processes explained earlier to empower the doer of the task at the lowest level are not top-down processes. All these processes are structured so that the employee realizes that he or she is choosing to follow them, not because he or she is being told to but because of his or her own benefit. That is the only way these processes stand a chance for successful implementation.

Also, there is no supervision, as such, to check or monitor whether these processes are being implemented. There is a tendency to micromanage a new process implementation. You, as a leader, should in no way become a micromanager. To avoid becoming one, we are laying out a process to lead right.

Process for Leading Right

Mindset: Inspire, not motivate.

The most important thing to understand is that the leader's role is to inspire, not motivate. Motivation, to be long lasting, has to come from within. The employee has to bring the motivation with them, day in and day out. It is easier if the employee can see the big picture and draw a line of sight from the day-to-day tasks to the success of the company. We laid out a process step in chapter 3 while going over the process of owning the tasks. Sometimes, the employee will not be able to see the big picture. That is when that leader takes on the role of providing inspiration. Inspire, not motivate should become the motto.

Task: Provide meaning regularly

Providing inspiration should be organic and natural. It should be done regularly as a process. Marshall Goldsmith provides a structure for this in his book, *Triggers: Creating Behavior That Lasts –Becoming the Person You Want to Be.* The structure is shown as an example of how Alan Mullaly, CEO of Ford Motor company, opens up his leadership meeting every time in the same fashion.

We think that the same structure should be followed where, in every weekly status meeting, the purpose of the project should be reviewed. The same words should not be repeated, but the essence of the project should be reviewed to provide the contextual meaning as to why the work is being done.

Measurement: Team morale

When you inspire by providing meaning regularly, you will see a morale improvement within your team. You should survey the team to know how the morale of the team has increased.

Action steps for this process

Here is the summary of action steps needed to implement the process for leading right.

- Mindset change in understanding that a leader's role is to inspire.
- Provide meaning regularly through a structured way
- Measure the team morale

Results to Be Expected

From time immemorial, there have been hundreds of books written on leadership. We have read quite a few of these leadership books. We tried to distill the essence of leadership in a few sentences. In our opinion, leadership at the line-manager level is the most critical form of leadership. At the danger of repeating ourselves, we have to remind you that most work, if not all work, happens at the lowest level of the organization. Who will these employees interact with on a regular basis? It is their manager or the project manager.

If the manager or the project manager leads the team right by following a very simple process of inspiring, providing meaning, and measuring the team morale, the leader takes himself or herself out as a factor contributing to the disengagement of the employee. That is a very significant improvement. It is so significant that it will help tasks get done faster exponentially. Imagine that!

CHAPTER 12

SET PRIORITIES

"A man is not idle because he is absorbed in thought. There is visible labor and there is invisible labor."

– Victor Hugo

Situation: Missing Priorities

When someone works on a task way before it is needed or way after it is needed, then most likely, it was not known which tasks were dependent on which tasks. When the dependent tasks are not known and the task is completed, then most likely, that task was not the right task to work on.

For example, a team repairs a road that was full of potholes. In a week, a different team comes and digs up the road to fix the telephone lines or water pipes or something, thus causing the first teams work to go to waste. Now, the road will be back to full of potholes. This was the state of affairs growing up in India, whenever a road was repaired, like clockwork, the very next week or so it used to be dug up for one valid reason or the other, leaving potholes most of the time. Repairing a road was not a small matter with all the bureaucracy then, and similarly, digging up a hole was also not a small matter. In either situation, a lot of planning would have happened, but it so happens one team did not know the dependency it had on another, causing havoc to the roads that were already in a bad shape to begin with. That was then, but things for sure would have improved by now.

The above example shows how a task done earlier than it should be can cause rework.

On the other side, is the task that gets done later than planned. Not because of some delay, but because the doer of the task did not know it was needed earlier. This is a straightforward miss but it happens more often than expected.

The root cause of this situation is not having the right set of priorities. It is the primary responsibility of the project manager to make sure the tasks are lined up right and prioritized so everyone is working on the right task.

Here is the process for setting priorities

Process for Setting Priorities

Mindset: Accountable

Setting priorities for the tasks is the leader's responsibility. We outlined a process for individual contributors to prioritize tasks. That process is when there are multiple tasks from multiple projects. For a specific project, the priorities need to be set by the leader. If everything is a priority, then nothing is a priority. If nothing is a priority, then the most important task is not the one that will be worked on, almost all the time. One of the biggest challenges, as we mentioned before, is that because of conflicting priorities, unimportant and not so urgent task is worked on, most of the time. Which means the doer of the task sees conflicting priorities and decides to work on something that is a Quadrant 4 task.

The mindset change that needs to happen is that at no point in time will there be two #1 priorities. There can only be one #1 priority at any point of time. The leader has to take accountability of prioritizing and own this responsibility.

Task to perform: Communicate the process to the team

The leader has to communicate to the team that if there are two #1 Priorities at any point in time, then it is his or her failure as a leader. So, here is the process that needs to be followed. In the very first meeting with the team, the leader has to declare the following.

- I am accountable for setting priorities.
- I will set only one # 1 priority at any point in time.
- I will have failed as your leader if you have two #1 priorities at any point in time.
- There is a big white space between #1 priority and #2 priority and I, as the leader, take up that white space between #1 priority and #2 priority.
- You cannot jump from #1 priority to #2 priority without completing #1 priority.
- If you have to jump from #1 priority to #2 priority, then you have to notify me before jumping, and not after.

With these declarations, it will be clear to the team members that #1 priority should not be taken lightly. It will also make them realize that, as a leader, your job is to know the big picture to the full extent and also understand the moving parts and so they will allow, willingly, for you to set the priorities. Also, when priorities change, which happens all the time, the communications happen so the priorities are adjusted prior to them being worked on. Knowing that someone has not worked on the #1 priority in a status call or in a report is a reactive way of knowing, and there is nothing that you can do about that after the fact.

Measurement: Number of priority changes

It is a valuable metric to know how many times a #1 priority task changes after work commences. If the priority changes happen often, then there is a chance that the doer of the task can get disengaged.

Action steps for this process

Here is the summary of action steps needed to implement the process for setting priorities.

- Mindset change in understanding that a leader is accountable for setting priorities and cannot set two #1 priorities at the same time
- Communicate clearly the process of how priorities work.
- Measure the number of priority changes

Results to Be Expected

Shifting priorities, as well as missing priorities, cause not just wastage of time but also cause disengagement. Project deliverables are postponed when priorities shift. If the priorities shift regularly, then the team cannot work with the sense of urgency that is needed to complete the deliverables on time, because they are waiting for the priorities to again shift.

CHAPTER 13

PROMOTE A CULTURE OF RECOGNIZING GREAT WORK

"When I was a kid, I had a tendency to criticize. But when I did, my mum would whisk me off to the bathroom to stand in front of a mirror. Ten minutes, never less. To think about how criticism is a poor reflection on the one who criticizes."

– Richard Branson

Situation: How to Motivate

The classical Carrots-and-Sticks approach has proven to work in the short-term but not in the long-term as a motivator. There have been many studies done to prove it. To illustrate our point, we took only couple of references from Daniel Pink's book, *Drive: The Surprising Truth About What Motivates Us*.

The first reference is a story from the well-known novel, *The Adventures of Tom Sawyer* written by Mark Twain. It is the story of how Tom Sawyer turns the drudgery of work (whitewashing a fence) into play and makes a fortune as well as discovering a great human law.

> "Tom gave up the brush with reluctance in his face, but alacrity in his heart. And while the late steamer Big Missouri worked and sweated in the sun, the retired artist sat on a barrel in the shade close by, dangled his legs, munched his apple, and planned the slaughter of more innocents. There was no lack of material; boys happened along every little while; they came to jeer, but remained to whitewash. By the time Ben was fagged out, Tom had traded the next chance to Billy Fisher for a kite, in good repair; and when *he* played out, Johnny Miller bought in for a dead rat and a string to swing it with – and so on, and so on, hour after hour. And when the middle of the afternoon came, from being a poor poverty-stricken boy in the morning, Tom was literally rolling in wealth. He had besides the things before mentioned, twelve marbles, part of a jews-harp, a piece of blue bottle-glass to look through, a spool cannon, a key that wouldn't unlock anything, a fragment of chalk, a glass stopper of a decanter, a tin soldier, a couple of tadpoles, six fire-crackers, a kitten with only one eye, a brass door-knob, a

dog-collar – but no dog – the handle of a knife, four pieces of orange-peel, and a dilapidated old window sash.

The moral of this story is captured in this sentence.

> "Work consists of whatever a body is *obliged* to do, and that Play consists of whatever a body is not obliged to do"

This is the reason given for why Wikipedia is a success, whereas Microsoft failed at creating MSN Encarta (remember that?) failed.

Here is the second reference. The London School of Economics reviewed 51 studies done inside of companies on pay-for-performance plans. Their conclusion, after reviewing all these studies, was that financial incentives resulted in a negative impact of overall performance. Negative Impact!

If you have not come across any of these studies and still hold the idea that carrots-and-stick approach works, then please listen to Dan Pink's Ted Talks if you are short on time. If you have more time, then read his book, *Drive*. There is another book, *Carrots and Sticks: Unlock the Power of Incentives to Get Things Done*, written by Ian Ayres, which shows in a very humorous way how to use incentives, not in the regular way that we know of, but in a whole different way to get things done. It is the same principle in action though.

Process for Promoting a Culture of Recognizing Great Work

Mindset: Understand what not to do and what to do

Understanding that financial incentives don't work in the long-term and also understanding that manipulating like how Tom Sawyer did can only work short-term is the mental shift that is needed. These are the things that will not work, and there are plenty of studies to prove it. Now, that is what not to do. What has shown to work is "Peer-to-Peer" recognition.

Peer-to-Peer recognition has been proven as the most effective way of keeping teams engaged. Ken Blanchard's book title proclaims this principle. "Help People Reach Their Full Potential. Catch Them Doing Something Right."

Our suggestion is that you go an extra step. You enable your entire team to make a daily habit of catching folks doing something right. Setting up a process so that peer-to-peer recognition happens regularly is a very important part of cultivating a high-performing team

Task: Make a ritual

In our projects, we usually create an online forum where folks can recognize each other's work. The online forum can be a SharePoint site or an online blog where people can say nice things about each other. Most of the time, it is the downstream person who appreciates work done by the upstream person. For example, a developer may thank the systems analyst for the nicely done detailed technical document or a tester appreciating the coder for on-time code delivery. Peer-to-peer recognition in its simplest form!

A better way to promote peer-to-peer recognition is to create an outlet for easy retrieval of these peer recognitions. What we mean is that most peer recognitions get hidden after they are delivered. If you can maintain an online forum similar to that of LinkedIn, where referrals stay forever, it keeps the team morale up. For example, if a team member is down because of some issue, then he can open up his online wall of recognition and perk himself up. An instant elevation of mood! This is the power of peer-to-peer recognition. So, make it a point to not get accolades buried in emails.

Here are some steps that you can take to make peer-to-peer recognition part of your team's culture.

- Give out a weekly high-performer award. The team nominates and selects the high-performer. You will not play any role in selecting or nominating the high-performer.
- Make it easier for peer-to-peer recognition to happen openly and on a daily basis. It is better to setup up an online place instead of email because email gets buried.
- Usually work moves from one team member to another, so during this process have the downstream team member find something to recognize in the work done by the upstream team member. The recognition can be

for the quality of the work done or can even be for simple things.
- Recognize the people who provide peer-to-peer recognition. We have awards for folks who have recognized their peers the most.

When peer-to-peer recognition becomes a daily practice, the team transforms into a highly motivated, highly engaged, and high-performing team.

Measurement: Know your recognizers

One metric that we used to closely follow was the number of people who recognize others more frequently. The person who is being recognized is definitely getting credit but the person doing the recognizing should also get credit. The idea is to promote a culture of recognizing great work, and it can flourish only if there are more people recognizing. So, you need to pay close attention to people who are frequent recognizers and make sure they are recognized too.

Action steps for this process

Here is the summary of action steps needed to implement the process for setting priorities.

- Mindset change in understanding that pay-for-performance does not work in the long-term, and peer-to-peer recognition is the most effective way of motivating teams

- Make it a ritual to catch someone doing right, and practice that ritual daily if possible.
- Measure not just who gets more recognition but who recognizes most to promote the culture of peer-to-peer recognition.

Results to Be Expected

Once peer-to-peer recognition becomes a regular practice, you now have a team that is self-powered. It does not need any external motivation or external correction or external regulation. Now, you will have a team that is as close to self-managing as it can be.

Self-managing teams is a relatively new concept. Very few companies have tried and succeeded at self-management. As of the writing of this book, Zappos is trying this concept out. Self-management is being rolled out in Zappos, where Tony Shieh, the CEO of Zappos is promoting self-management by removing all managers. His company is supposedly following the model proposed in the book, *Holocracy: The New Management System For The Rapidly Changing World*.

Only time will tell if many companies will adopt this new way of managing teams. Until then, having a high-performing team that is fully engaged, self-motivated, and self-regulated is the best thing that you can hope for as a leader.

CHAPTER 14

FACILITATE GREAT WORK

"There's as much crookedness as you want to find. There was something Abraham Lincoln said - he'd rather trust and be disappointed than distrust and be miserable all the time. Maybe I trusted too much."

– John Wooden

Situation: Right Person not Working on the Right Task

Imagine for a moment that you have a trusted system to manage tasks, and that you know what the right task is. Now, how can you assign this task to the right person? Before knowing who the right person is to work on the right task, we need to explain what we mean by the right person. The best way to explain this is to give a first-hand example from a program manager who saw a program unravel in front of his eyes because the right persons were not assigned. So, here is the story in his words.

> "I worked closely on a program that was the company's # 1 program to move our company into a new strategic direction. The company had partnered with two clients to make a new product and the plan was to get more clients in a year or so. It was a very exciting time for our company and for the clients because of the potential of this new product, which leveraged the technical expertise of our company and the business process knowledge of our clients. There were many issues with the way the program started and the way it was run but to keep it relevant to the subject matter, the biggest issue that I saw was the assignment of the resources.
>
> The consulting division of our company was managing the program and the primary concern for this division was to bill the client as much as we could. So, our critical technical resources, who could have helped move our technical work forward, were assigned to the client to support them in understanding the technical aspect of the product. In other words, the technical resources were working in an advisory role instead of doing the technical work. This assignment neither helped the project nor the client nor the resources. This issue was brought to the Program Director multiple times but the Program Director came from a consulting background and was convinced

that it was the smartest thing to do because we were billing the client. The reasoning was that if we did not give these resources to the client then our client will get someone internally which will not get us the billing dollars.

To make matters worse, we did not have the right resources available to work on our project since most resources were assigned to other critical projects. To fix this issue, our consulting division had another brilliant idea to increase billing. You see, our company had started a pilot program of training fresh graduates and the first batch of these trainees was available. Our management convinced the clients that these resources were well trained and also cheap. So, these new bees were assigned to the most strategic program of our company.

However, nothing was inherently wrong with assigning new bees except the balance was out of whack. You cannot have 90% rookies and expect to win Super Bowl. If it was one game then, maybe, you could but not Super Bowl with that kind of ratio. With that ratio of new bees to seniors, the seniors were not able to handle the requests for work or review the work of the rookies. So, work either got delayed or was of low quality.

The third place where the assignments were done wrong was in the PMO. The PMO was run by a top management-consulting firm, which was initially brought in to audit the program but stayed on to run the PMO. The management-consulting firm may have had the expertise to set-up and run the PMOs but the team assigned to the program did not have that expertise. There was an incident in a management meeting where the team lead from the consulting firm was looking at the MS Project Schedules of a project and asked a question of what Resource A [50%] and Resource B [25%] meant. He did not seem to have worked on any Project scheduling tool before and that's when the top management realized that they were paying top dollar for someone who did not know the basics of project management.

With all these improper resource assignments and other stuff, the program went through major issues; also the clients went their separate ways. I came off the program too but later on came to know that the scope was cut down and it took much longer to deliver that reduced scope."

From the above anecdote, the main lesson learned is that the resource assignments were not done in the best interests of the project. Sometime, you spend the top dollar, but don't get the right resources because you made the wrong assumption. Sometimes, you try to save money and hope against hope that things will go your way. In these scenarios, or other similar scenarios, the end result is the same where the right person is not assigned to the task. After all, for large projects, there may be many factors influencing the resource assignment. However, the same end result can come true for smaller projects or personal tasks.

For example, if you are a control freak, then you may want to do every task by yourself. You may not have developed the discipline to delete a task if not needed, delegate a task if someone else can do it or defer a task if you can do this task at an appropriate time. If you are not a control freak but have worked with one, then you probably know what we are talking about. Especially, if the control freak is your manager. We have come across managers who hire highly paid, highly talented people and then micromanage them to the detriment of the project.

Process for Facilitating Great work

Mindset change: Understand the difference between Bad Work Versus Good Work Versus Great work

We are taking the definitions of Bad Work, Good Work, and Great Work from Michael Bungay Stanier's book *Do More Great Work: Stop the Busywork. Start the Work That Matters*, which illustrates so well the differences between these three.

"Bad Work

Bad Work is a waste of time, energy, and life. Doing it once is one time too many. This is not something to be polite about. It's not something to be resigned to. This is work that is pointless.

Good Work

Good Work is the familiar, useful, productive work you do— and you likely do it well. You probably spend most of your time on Good Work, and there's nothing wrong with that. Good Work blossoms from your training, your education, and the path you've traveled so far. All in all, it's a source of comfort, nourishment, and success.

There's a range of Good Work: At one end it's engaging and interesting work; at the other, it is more mundane but you recognize its necessity and are happy enough to spend some time doing it

Great Work

Great Work is what we all want more of. This is the work that is meaningful to you, that has an impact and makes a difference. It inspires, stretches, and provokes. Great Work is the work that matters.

It is a source of both deep comfort and engagement— often you feel as if you're in the "flow zone," where time stands still and you're working at your best, effortlessly. The comfort comes from its connection, its "sight line," to what is most meaningful to you— not only your core values, and beliefs, but also your aspirations and hopes for the impact you want to have on the world."

In short, great work is something you can't stop talking about, even in social situations outside of work. Good work is something you do really well, but at the end of the week you cannot usually remember what you worked on. Bad work is something that drains your energy, even though you may be good at this type of work.

Task: Help them choose their task

The best thing to facilitate great work is to let your team member choose their task. We might have lost some of the leaders with the above statement, but stay with us because we will make a case for it.

As shown earlier, the Tom Sawyer effect is real. Work can become play if it is chosen. Another example is taken from John Wooden, the renowned basketball coach, who won 10 NCAA Basketball championships. John Wooden was not just a successful coach in basketball but his philosophy called *Pyramid of Success* became a hit in business circles. In one of his many leadership seminars, Coach Wooden gave examples of how leaders can miss great talent if they do not let their team members volunteer. There was one instance of how a player who did not show great talent in practice became a star player in games, after pleading to become a starter.

It is not uncommon in sports for that to happen. Tom Brady, New England Patriots quarterback who has won 4 NFL championships (so far) tying the most championships won by a quarterback, was never a starter to begin with.

Assisting your team member to volunteer for tasks can help in turning around some projects. Needless to say, you have to implement this process with great care by measuring and monitoring.

Measurement: Know the % of great work done per week.

Help your team members follow this process to measure and improve.

The first thing to do is to take stock of these tasks and categorize them. Create a list of all the tasks that you have done in the last week and the ones that are coming up. Basically, take a two-week stock of tasks and list all of them. In this list, include the tasks as well as the support tasks for these tasks. For example, if you have a task to prepare a report then include as tasks, the meetings, the emails, and the research you need to do to complete this task.

The second thing is to do a quick estimate of the time it takes to do each of these tasks. Note the time against these tasks in a separate column. This can be a rough estimate, and does not need to be very accurate.

The third thing to do is categorize each of these tasks as great work, good work, or bad work. For example, here is a sample of what your list could look like.

Tasks	Estimate	Type of work
Task 1 - Actual	10 hours	Good
Task 1 - Meetings	2 hours	Great
Task 1 - Emails	1 hour	Bad
Task 1- Research	2 hour	Good
Task 2 - Actual	20 hours	Great
Task 2 - Meetings	10 hours	Bad
Task 2 - Research	5 hours	Good
Task 3 – Research	30 hours	Bad

In this sample of 80 hours of work, 41 hours were bad, 17 were good, and 22 were great; which means the majority of tasks were bad work. your team member will be able to know the breakdown of bad work vs good work vs great work.

To get started on doing great work, you need to know what is great work and what percentage of great work are you currently doing. As explained above, here are the steps you need to do to understand the percentage of great work.

- Make a list of tasks from the current week and the next week.
- Review your calendar and email to add to this list the support tasks that you have done for the above tasks.
- Add these support tasks to the task list.
- Estimate how much time you took/will take to complete each of these tasks.
- Enter these estimates in a separate column.
- In a new column, categorize each task as bad, goo, or great.
- Total the estimated time on each of these task categories, and calculate the percentages of bad, good, or great work to understand your percentage of great work.

We know that some weeks are different from others, and so the percentage of great work that you have calculated may not be indicative of the great work that you typically do. However, by doing this exercise every week, you can observe the trend of how the percentage of great work is improving from week to week.

Action steps for this process

Here is the summary of action steps needed to implement the process of facilitating great work.

- Mindset change in understanding the differences of bad work versus good work versus great work so as to figure out the quality of work being done by your team.
- Assist your team members in choosing their task as much as possible within the constraints of the project.
- Measure the progress made from week to week in improvement in the percentage of great work

Results to Be Expected

The core idea behind this process is that there is a possibility that no one knows better than himself or herself what great work means and is for him or her. Finding star performers makes a huge difference in the success and failure of a project. One of the processes of finding your star performers is to let them choose their task, which will help them do great work.

Imagine the benefit to your team and to your project if you can turn every team member into a high-performer.

CHAPTER 15

ELIMINATE BAD MEETINGS

"If you had to identify, in one word, the reason why the human race has not achieved, and never will achieve, its full potential, that word would be 'meetings."

– Dave Barry

Situation: Bad Meetings

Many meetings are bad but not all meetings are bad. There is a great benefit to meetings. Having said that, there are a lot of bad meetings happening on a regular basis. Many leaders go from meeting to meeting and spend almost their entire day going from one bad meeting to another. Many leaders pull people into meetings that suck the energy out of the workplace.

We advocate that meetings are a great benefit if they are run properly. They are many reasons why meetings are not run properly, and we will go through 3 of these.

- Inviting people who are not needed in the meeting
- Mixing up the subjects
- Checking out of meetings

Inviting people who are not needed in the meeting is the same mentality displayed when doing a reply all. A reply all seems so convenient, even though it wastes the time and energy of the person who is unnecessarily carbon copied. Carbon copying had become such a big problem for some companies that they had to start a movement called "Death to CC" to reduce the unnecessary reply all and carbon copying in emails. The same mentality is in play when inviting anyone and everyone to a meeting without paying close attention to who is not needed in a meeting.

The issue is on both sides too, the invitee and the invited. The invited come to the meeting without understanding the purpose and the agenda of the meeting. It is like getting on a bus without knowing where the bus is going. In real life, not many sane people do that, but in work life, it is common for folks to attend a meeting for which they have no value to add nor any value to receive.

The second problem is mixing up the subjects. Attention is not paid as to why you should not have a brainstorming meeting in the middle of a status meeting. A status meeting is meant to track the progress being made, and if a concern is raised, then you need to table that concern to be discussed separately and not shift the meeting's purpose to brainstorm the solution. The segregation is not followed.

The third problem is when people check out of meetings because they are multitasking, or skip the meeting altogether because of an assumed principle that "all meetings are optional." There was an innovative and transformational effort pioneered in Best Buy called R.O.W.E (Results Oriented Work Environment), where one of the items on its manifesto was that "All meetings are optional." Checking out of meetings because you do not think the meeting is not important is not the right way to handle the issue of bad meetings.

Here is our process to stop bad meetings happening in the first place.

Process for Eliminating Bad Meetings

Mindset: Understand the types of meetings

If you categorize all the different types of meetings, then you can broadly classify them into 2 types of meetings.

- Working sessions/Group tasks
- Information sharing/Status meetings

Any meeting where actual work is done like planning, brainstorming or decision-making or issue resolving or risk-mitigating, fall into the first category of working sessions. These working sessions can be called group tasks, as the only reason that these meetings are called is for moving one or more project tasks forward.

The second type of meeting is information sharing, whether it is training, status giving, or status gathering.

When these two types of meeting are combined knowingly or unknowingly, it causes the meetings to turn into bad meetings and get derailed.

Task: Structure the project meetings

The assumption here is that the leader (Project Manager/Manager/Program Manager) is leading the project meetings and also setting the direction for the other meetings happening on the project. So, the leader can control all aspects of the meetings. With this assumption, we can determine the structure of every meeting on the project. The steps to follow on these meetings are:

- Do not combine the two types of meetings, because for information sharing meetings, you can stay on point and time and wrap up the meeting. Whereas group tasks, must be given the time and the attention to finish.
- Every group task attendee should add value to the discussion and also should come prepared to the

meeting. For that reason, all relevant material must be shared well before the meeting.
- At the beginning of the group task, every attendee should be surveyed to find out how much time was spent on the material, if there was any. If more than 25% of attendees did not spend any time on the material, then the group task should be postponed.
- If multiple items are being worked on in a group task, then these items should be prioritized so that the most important item is worked on first and given the full attention and time. The underlying assumption will be that if all the items are not covered, then either the group task will be extended or a follow-up scheduled.
- Status meetings should be eliminated if status can be collected and displayed automatically through your project management systems. If a discussion needs to happen on status, then it is because there is an issue and not for purely sharing information. Imagine the amount of time you can give back if you eliminated status meetings.

Measurement: Know the time saved

As you make the mindset change and structure your meetings, you will start seeing your calendar open up. Measure the current state of your meetings, the time saved as well as the quality of the meetings after you put the process in place. Make necessary adjustments based on the data to improve the quality or the time saved.

Action Steps for this process

Here is the summary of action steps needed to implement the process of eliminating bad meetings.

- Mindset change in understanding the two types of meetings and why these should not be combined.
- Structure your meetings so that every attendee is accounted for and prepared for your meetings.
- Measure the time saved week to week by eliminating bad meeting, and also measure the improvement in the quality of the existing meetings.

Results to Be Expected

Following the action steps laid here can eliminate the major problems of bad meetings.

Imagine if everyone in the meeting had value to add or gain from the meeting. It will not be like people getting on a bus without knowing where the bus is going. So much wastage of time will be eliminated.

Imagine if everyone came prepared to the meeting. With the time saved from not going to unnecessary meetings, folks will now have time to go through the meeting material and prepare themselves. Now, actual work can be done in meetings. You will not hear people end the meetings by saying, "Now, let's go do some actual work," implying the meetings were a waste of time.

MANAGE. LEAD. TRANSFORM.

Imagine if meetings were treated as critical part of work getting done. There would be so much energy and collaboration. Needless to say, tasks will be done way quicker that you were used to.

CHAPTER 16

FROM LEADING TO TRANSFORMING

"Motivation and inspiration energize people, not by pushing them in the right direction as control mechanisms do but by satisfying basic human needs for achievement, a sense of belonging, recognition, self-esteem, a feeling of control over one's life, and the ability to live up to one's ideals. Such feelings touch us deeply and elicit a powerful response."

– John Kotter

The 5 Team processes

In part 2 of this book, the team processes that we have laid out are:

1. Lead Right
2. Set Priorities
3. Promote a Culture of Recognizing Great Work
4. Facilitate Great Work
5. Eliminate Bad Meetings

By implementing these 5 processes, the leader guarantees cultivating a high-performing team. Since projects by their nature have an end date, the teams that come together have to disperse at the end of the project. But the principles and feelings of great work done by each of these teams will remain in memory, and the teams will want to recreate this in all of their future projects. So, as a leader, you may start to have a following of team members who will want to work with you in your future projects.

It is a hallmark of great leaders to have a following. We guarantee that it will happen to you. You will also be asked to present these processes to other project managers. Who does not want a high-performing team, right?

Are you ready for the Next Stage?

In the first stage, as the project manager, you managed the tasks by implementing the 7 processes of the Manage stage.

The implementation was neither forced nor mandated. For the implementation to be successful, it needed a hands-off approach. That is how you started. By slowly and steadily influencing your team in practicing the steps needed to gain the benefits of a trusted system, you managed through that stage.

After the first stage, you entered the second stage where you could take the processes to the next level, to the team level from the individual level. Successful implementation of these 5 processes will now move your tasks and project way faster than you imagined. The team morale is up, and the project has turned around. We showed how a high-performing team could turn things around by identifying risks and stopping them from becoming issues. It is huge to not have crippling issues on the project. Obviously, your project has turned around and is being noticed by senior management.

We know that as individuals and teams within an organization start doing great work, it will bubble up and get noticed. As a leader, you will now be asked to disclose your secret. That is when you bring these processes and the following processes forward to your senior management.

What is the fun if only one or two projects get done within 50% or less time? The fun is when every project in your organization gets done within 50% or less time. Imagine if you are responsible for that. You may feel that it is outside of your comfort zone, but we hope this quote from Seth Godin from his book *Linchpin: Are you indispensable?* can get you ready for the next stage.

"Discomfort brings engagement and change. Discomfort means you're doing something that others were unlikely to do, because they're hiding out in the comfortable zone. When your uncomfortable actions lead to success, the organization rewards you and brings you back for more."

The Next Stage

The next stage is the Transform stage, where the processes at the organization level will be laid out so that every task and every person in an organization can be aligned with the goals of the company. By taking the successes of implementing processes at the individual and team level to the organization level, this will start moving the entire organization at a faster speed. Faster speed of completing the tasks - the lowest level of tasks.

PART 3 – TRANSFORM

"Without execution, the breakthrough thinking breaks down, learning adds no value, people don't meet their stretch goals, and the revolution stops dead in its tracks. What you get is change for the worse, because failure drains the energy from your organization. Repeated failure destroys it."

– Larry Bossidy

CHAPTER 17

ESTABLISH A RALLYING CRY

"To succeed consistently, good managers need to be skilled not just in choosing, training, and motivating the right people for the right job, but in choosing, building, and preparing the right organization for the job as well."

– Clayton M. Christensen

Situation: Broken at the Top

We have established the fact that project failure is common. The purpose of doing any project at the most basic level is to either save money or to make money for the company. In other words, projects are started to improve the bottom-line of the company. Every company strives for that goal, and when projects fail, the company goals are not met.

At your company the situation could be that the organization seems to be moving in different directions at different speeds. It may feel like fish trapped in a net. It may be because of a lack of common motivation, a rallying cry.

At the top-most level, there needs to be a "Rallying Cry," as Patrick Lencioni says in his book *The Advantage*. A rallying cry is something that everyone in the organization can get aligned to: everyone from top to bottom of an organization. Patrick Lencioni provides a concise definition as shown below:

> *"To avoid politics and turf battles, leaders must establish a rallying cry - a single overriding theme that remains the top priority of the entire leadership team for a given period of time. In turn, this rallying cry or "thematic goal" serves to align employees throughout the organization and provides an objective tool for resetting direction when things get out of sync."*

If there is no rallying cry/thematic goal/WIG (Wildly Important Goal like Stephen Covey puts it) that everyone in the company understands and follows, then that is the first thing to do.

Establishing a rallying cry is the necessary step, whether it is for a big company or for a small company. This can apply for a project, or for a family or even for an individual person. To get a sense of urgency and to focus the efforts in a particular direction, there can be one area or aspect that needs transformational change – be it in a large organization or with one single individual. Having said that, here is the process to implement a process for establishing a rallying cry.

Process for Establishing a Rallying Cry

Mindset: Derive Meaning

Understand that every employee should be able to derive the correct meaning from the rallying cry. This is of critical importance. So, the wording of the rallying cry should not have any potential for misinterpretation.

Task: Figure out the keystone habit

A keystone habit can cause a chain reaction of positive change across many different areas of work, as well as life. Here are a couple of examples taken from Charles Duhigg's book *The Power of Habit: Why We Do What We Do In Life and Business*

- **Family Dinners**: "Families who habitually eat dinner together seem to raise children with better homework skills, higher grades, greater emotional control, and more confidence."
- **Making your bed**: "Bed makers are also more likely to like their jobs, own a home, exercise regularly, and feel well rested."

As you can see, a keystone habit in one area can transcend into multiple areas and make things better. We tried this approach in our projects. We picked up meeting minutes as a keystone habit to improve in all the projects in our PMO. The reason to pick this as a keystone habit was that no project manager was going to complain about meeting minutes as a tough thing to do. It also took very little amount of time to do meeting minutes.

The process that we implemented was that every meeting should have a minimum of two action items. If there were no action items, then at least one decision should have been made. What is the purpose of meeting if there are no action items or decisions that come out of that meeting? This simple change of documenting meeting minutes in this format caused a positive chain reaction of action items getting done on time as fewer and fewer balls were dropped. This habit also influenced risks, issues, and decisions getting logged and resolved. It also helped in the project schedules being maintained on a weekly basis.

Measurement: Decide on the duration

For a rallying cry to be successful, it should be temporary. It should be for a limited term. The duration has to be tweaked till you get it right. Some keystone habits may take longer, and so these need to be researched, and the benchmarks known before deciding on the duration.

Action Steps for this process

Here is the summary of action steps needed to implement the process for establishing a rallying cry.

- Mindset change in understanding that every employee should be able to derive the correct meaning from the rallying cry.
- Figure out a keystone habit that can have the potential to cause a chain reaction of positive changes across the organization.
- Decide on the duration for the rallying cry to exist by measuring successes of other keystone habits.

Results to Be Expected

Here is an example of how a rallying cry can transform a corporation.

In 1987, Paul O'Neill was appointed Chairman and CEO of the Pittsburg industrial giant Alcoa, The Aluminum Company of America. In his first speech to the investors of the company, he made a rallying cry for worker safety. He mentioned that his goal was to go for zero injuries, because many employees were getting injured so badly that they were missing work. O'Neill's rallying cry met with significant resistance from his board of directors as well as investors. Some investors ordered Alcoa stock to be sold immediately because they thought the focus of the top-ranking official of the company was not on profits but on worker safety.

However, this rallying cry resonated inside the company and started a chain reaction of positive change. Who could argue against worker safety, right? What kind of a manager or employee would not get behind such a meaningful and powerful rallying cry, especially when he/she would have come across an injury to one of their workers, or even themselves. The effect of this rallying cry also reflected positively on the profits. Here is an excerpt from Charles Duhigg's book *The Power of Habit: Why We Do What We Do In Life and Business*

> "Within a year of O'Neill's speech, Alcoa's profits would hit a record high. By the time O'Neill retired in 2000 to become Treasury Secretary, the company's annual net income was five times larger than before he arrived, and its market capitalization had risen by $27 billion. Someone who invested a million dollars in Alcoa on the day O'Neill was hired would have earned another million dollars in dividends while he headed the company, and the value of their stock would be five times bigger when he left.
>
> What's more, all that growth occurred while Alcoa became one of the safest companies in the world."

In your case, the results may be different but definitely positive to move your organization, as a whole, in the right direction.

CHAPTER 18

ALIGN STRATEGIC INITIATIVES

"If your goal is anything but profitability - if it's to be big, or to grow fast, or to become a technology leader - you'll hit problems."

– Michael Porter

Situation: Strategic Initiatives not Aligned

What is a Strategic Initiative?

"A Strategic Initiative (SI) is a program or even a project if it is a small company that has the potential, if successfully completed, to transform the organization in a beneficial way, as intended by the rallying cry."

In other words, Strategic Initiatives are usually groups of projects or groups of program, depending on the size of the company. With this definition, any strategic initiative has to draw the meaning from the rallying cry. A strategic initiative should seamlessly align with the rallying cry. It must not feel contrived. Also, it should be directionally true.

Most companies have a problem with aligning their Strategic Initiatives to ongoing projects. Sometimes, there are projects that go on for years that have no link to the current Strategic Initiatives.

Some companies take a lot of time to roll-out goals to the lowest level. A Fortune 50 company rolled out the goals for that year to all its employees by the end of the second quarter. That was not the first or last time that this company rolled out the goals so late. That is not acceptable.

Both of these problems contribute to a situation where multiple issues show up at the organizational level.

- Poor decision making at the top-level.
- Lack of focus on the SIs.
- No sense of urgency.
- Demotivates engaged employees.
- Success of the initiatives will be limited.

Process for Aligning the Strategic Initiatives

Mindset: Limit the Strategic Initiatives

You need to have strategic initiatives of 4 to 6, maximum. Anything more than that can cause an administrative nightmare in managing and focusing on these strategic initiatives.

Task: Use SMART framework

As with any program or a project, a strategic initiative should follow the SMART (Smart, Measurable, Attainable, Realistic and Timely) process to name the initiative. Any work or most work that anyone in the organization does can be linked to any one of these strategic initiatives. You may be wondering, why not call this a goal instead of a strategic initiative. The power is in the usage of the words.

A strategic initiative is not only a SMART goal, but also a powerful usage of the right words. If someone asks you as to what your goal is then you may say, "to lose weight," without thinking much. On the other hand, if someone asks you as to what your strategic initiative is then you will not blurt out "to lose weight," you will be specific in saying that your strategic initiative is "to lose 10 pounds by the end of the year." That is the power of words.

Measurement: Decide the CSFs, metrics and KPIs

What gets measured gets done. With this in mind the critical success factors (CSF) for the strategic initiatives should be decided first. Typically, the critical success factors of the strategic initiative will number 4 to 6, maximum. Usually, the primary success factors will be:

- Cost
- Scope
- Time
- Quality

And there could be some secondary success factors like:

- Customer satisfaction
- Safety
- Design

Once the critical success factors are decided, then the next step is to decide on the metrics and Key Performance Indicators (KPIs) for the strategic initiatives. This subject is vast, but instead of going into lots of details, the main things that need to be remembered when coming up with metrics and KPIs are as follows:

- What is a valuable metric to track on a particular Strategic Initiative (SI) may not be of same value for a different SI.
- Metrics must not be too difficult to measure. For instance, it should not take a Project Manager having to go through multiple information systems to get a metric. It could be too time-consuming and not give real time information.

- All KPIs are metrics, but not all metrics are KPIs.
- Metrics may not all be objective. There could be subjective metrics too.
- KPIs should be able to predict the outcomes so adjustments can be made to bring the SI back on track.

As mentioned earlier, what gets measured gets done but at the same time, what is difficult to measure and what is not needed to measure should also be taken into consideration before deciding on what to measure. The following process steps need to be performed to setup this process.

- Decide on 4 to 6 critical success factors.
- Choose the metrics that do not need any human touches to generate.
- Choose the KPIs that will give early warning signs for needed adjustments.
- Repeat the process as new strategic initiatives are added.

Once this process is set up, we need to make sure there is a process to cascade this information to the lowest level of the organization.

Action Steps for this process

Here is the summary of action steps needed to implement the process for aligning the strategic initiatives process.

- Identify not more than 4 to 6 strategic initiatives.
- Use the SMART framework to define these strategic initiatives and link the strategic initiatives to the rallying cry.
- Decide on the CSFs, Metrics, and KPIs.

Results to Be Expected

To see the expected results, it is critical that the SIs are cascaded down to the departments, teams, and individual contributors in a timely manner so that every piece of work that an employee does can be linked to the strategic initiatives.

The action steps that need to be performed in setting up the cascading process are as follows:

- Cascade down the calendar year SIs before the beginning. of the new year since most employees are enthusiastic at the beginning of the year.
- For mid-year SIs, the cascading must happen as soon as the SIs are defined and measurements put in place.
- Create programs or projects from the Sis, as these SIs cascade down the levels of the organization.
- Link every type of work that happens at the lower level to these projects or programs.

CHAPTER 19

SCHEDULE HEALTH CHECKUPS

"When people who are actually creating a system start to see themselves as the source of their problems, they invariably discover a new capacity to create results they truly desire."

– Peter M. Senge

Situation: Communications Breakdown

Communications breakdown can be common with teams working in silos. One project was late by 2 years simply because of communications breakdown. It took 3 years for this project to complete, and it was late by 2 years. That is not the sad part. The sad part was that the application that this project built was not needed anymore. Why? Because the company that funded the development of this application, on which thirty or so people were working to support their product, had stopped selling that product one year before the application was completed. Thirty people worked on something that was not needed. Pretty bad, right?

Imagine the lessons learned discussion, if there was one. To stop selling a product, you should be having discussions about why you should stop selling this product. You would have been analyzing sales data or something to make that decision. Which means, the decision to not sell the product could have been made maybe months before actually pulling the product from the market. During all these months, no one communicated to the development team to stop working on this application. How could this happen, right? This is a classic example of the work of a team of thirty people going to waste because of teams not talking to one another.

To avoid the communications breakdown, a process needs to be implemented to do regular health check-ups of Strategic Initiatives and the critical projects supporting these Initiatives.

Process for Scheduling Health Checkups of Projects

Mindset: It is not a witch-hunt

We have seen many health check-ups turn into witch-hunts. Even though the PMO explicitly may state that the health check-ups are not going to be witch-hunts, they ultimately turn into ones. There are many reasons for that. The primary reason is that these health check-ups are meant for senior management to resolve the issues of the project. Trust us, the project teams can resolve most of the problems themselves. The senior management should focus on the process, and help on the process if they see some breakdown of processes.

By focusing on the processes, and not so much on resolving the problems, the senior management can review more projects in less time. When the senior management tries to resolve the actual problems on the projects, then the health check-ups can easily become witch-hunts.

Task: Get the mix right

There is a tendency at the management level to only focus on the fires, so as to put them out. Any project that is not in trouble is not discussed in these health checkups. As mentioned earlier, this can turn into witch-hunts, and that is very demotivating. So, focus should be put on what is working as well as what is not working.

For that reason, there should be a good mix of Green Status projects along with Yellow and Red Status ones. There is another advantage from that. There could be something right that the Green Status projects are doing that can help the troubled projects.

Measurement: Not more than 2 meetings to attend

The maximum number of health check-ups per week or month that any employee should go to should be capped at two - one at the management level, and one at the individual contributor level. This should be measured to make sure that the balance is there, and that folks are not going from one status meeting to another.

Action Steps for this process

Here is the summary of action steps needed to implement the process for scheduling health check-ups.

- Avoid turning these health check-ups into witch-hunts.
- Have a mix of successful projects to discuss so that organizational learning is engendered.
- No more than 2 meetings per week per person.

Results to Be Expected

What works at the macro level can work at the micro level. Whether it is a large or a small organization, the processes will be the same. The complexity may increase, and so it may necessitate more coordination and more logistics to set up these processes, but the core principles are same. The core principles are:

1. Direction comes from the top in a timely fashion so that every individual's work is aligned to move the company in that direction, and
2. Regular check-ups help to course correct, so every piece of work contributes to the betterment of the company.

When the strategic initiatives are cascaded down to different levels of the organization, then more projects or programs may be created, and they will all have a hierarchical level under each of the strategic initiative.

CHAPTER 20

CONCLUSION: FROM TRANSFORMING TO TRANSCENDING

"Our intuition about the future is linear. But the reality of information technology is exponential, and that makes a profound difference. If I take 30 steps linearly, I get to 30. If I take 30 steps exponentially, I get to a billion"

– Ray Kurzweil

Exciting Times

These are exciting times to live in. There are so many innovations happening in every industry, where bigger and bolder projects are being attempted. Technological innovation is fuelling so many never-before-imagined projects like Going to Mars, Automated Cars, 3D printing, and Artificial Intelligence, to name just a few. The trend is that most projects have heavy technological component; in fact, every company can now be called a tech company, after how Uber, Airbnb, and Tesla have forced non-Tech companies to become Tech companies. So, most projects in the foreseeable future will have a heavy technological component to them. That is going to be very exciting for the future of project management.

With this excitement, also comes a challenge to every project manager to stay tuned into the advances being made for increasing the effectiveness of individuals, teams, and organizations. We will touch on these advances later in the chapter, but before that, we would like to recap the final processes of the MLT framework and talk about the problems of task management tools.

The Three Transforming Processes

The final 3 processes for the transforming an organization are as follows:

1. Establish a Rallying Cry.
2. Align Strategic Initiatives.
3. Schedule Health Check-ups.

These three leadership processes finish the connections that are needed from the lowest level to the highest level. As mentioned earlier, we have taken a bottom-up approach managing the lowest level of tasks, then leading with team processes, and finally transforming the organizational processes. We have seen that this process has a greater chance of success than the other way – the top-down approach, especially in larger companies.

Having said that, the top-down approach can be tried if your situation matches with any of the categories listed below.

Use a top-down approach if:

- You are a small company, and you think you can have better control with top-down approach
- You have tried the bottom-up earlier and did not succeed. So, now you want to switch things up and see if you can be successful
- Your company is undergoing a major shift in direction

Horse Before the Carriage

So far we have kept the discussion to processes, and none of these processes need any technology change. You do not need a new project management system or a new tool to implement any of the 15 processes of our system. We have seen many companies make huge investments in project management technology without taking the time to set up the right processes that are needed to get the work done in the right way. We believe that it is 90% processes and 10% tools. Implementing our MLT framework will surely reduce your project timelines by 50% or more.

Problems with Task Management Tools

There are hundreds of task management systems. The last time we counted, there were upwards of 500. New task management software applications keep coming up every year, and just this fact in itself may prove that there are gaps in current systems that these newer tools are trying to plug. These applications range from enterprise wide systems to stand-alone apps. For large companies, there are IT PPM enterprise wide systems like Oracle's Primavera, Microsoft Project Server, CA's Clarity, Planview, etc., and for the start-ups, there are cloud-based project management tools like Asana, Wrike, Smartsheet, Basecamp, Trello, etc.

We understand that grouping these systems of varying features into one umbrella called task management applications may not look and feel right. Some of these IT PPM enterprise systems will take months or years to implement with all the integrations into financial applications, whereas the cloud-based tools may not have as many features but are easier to implement. The only reason we are grouping them is because they are used in some form or another to plan, manage, and track tasks. If it helps, then think that we are grouping all vehicles, be it a bike or a space ship into one group – transportation systems.

With this variety of tools, there is definitely some confusion as to what will work best in your situation. Many companies take months to decide on the tool to implement, and then spend months or years to implement it. Just like the success rate of IT projects that we have seen earlier in chapter 1, these implementations also have the same potential for failure. So, it is very common to see companies move from one tool to another. Even Fortune 50 companies are sometimes forced to do that.

Recently, we came across a Fortune 50 company that was in the process of moving from Planview to Jira. The same company spent years trying to perfect their project management process through Planview, and they have now given up and are moving to Jira, even though Planview now has a cloud-based solution, Innotas. A startup that we know of moved from Wunderlist to Basecamp to Asana and then to Slack. Not happy with any of these tools, this startup is keeping some tasks on Basecamp, some on Asana, and using Slack for communications.

Obviously, it is not the lack of tools that is the cause. Despite a plethora of tools, managing tasks is still a huge problem, as shown by how mature companies as well as start-ups struggle with using the task management tool that works right for them. Also, each tool has its own set of problems. P3Alpha Consulting can help with finding the right project management tool for your situation. We know that the way work is getting done nowadays has changed a lot. A few years back, there was no Facebook, no WhatsApp, no Drop Box, no iPhone, etc. (Yes, it is difficult to imagine life without these.) There are some companies where the lifecycle of a task can follow these stages.

- Task is created in Google Docs
- Assigned in an email
- Clarified in Hangouts or skype

- Updated in a text
- Linked on Facebook for content
- Marked as done in WhatsApp

Each of these channels of communications is not specifically meant for managing tasks, but somehow it becomes so, either because of the ease of use or because of the preference of a team member. Also, when the team size increases, the preferences can be very dissimilar, increasing the number and complexity of the tools that interact with the task management tool.

We can help find the right solution for you in as difficult a scenario as shown above. We also keep track of all the advances being made in task management tools. We also guarantee that there is hope with the advances in Technology that will also impact the evolution of project management software.

The "Transcending" Stage

The advances in technologies like Voice Recognition, Machine Learning, Predictive Analytics, Cognitive Computing, just to name a few, will bring project management software into a new era. Combined with the right processes, the advances in productivity software, task management tools, and PPM (Project and Portfolio Management) software, the stage is set for Transcendence. In the transcending stage, the machine will make the decisions of assigning the right person to the right task, so that this task has the best chance of getting done in the right time.

Our company constantly monitors the advances being made in any related technologies that can help a project get done on time. We also update our processes to best use these advances in technology.

The right project management software can help you finish your projects way earlier than you ever have done before. If you need help with deciding or implementing project management software, please drop us an email at p3Alpha@p3alphaconsulting.com.

Final Thoughts

Before we say goodbye, we would like to mention that you, as a project manager, do not need to be frustrated or stuck in your career or leave project management altogether. We have seen many project managers' careers flounder without taking off. There is no need to solving the same project management problems again and again. There are solutions everywhere and in places where you sometimes least expect. So, have an open mind and remember that some solutions can be found outside of project management books. With that we will leave you with Tim Ferriss' quote from his book, *TOOLS OF TITIANS: THE TACTICS, ROUTINES, AND HABITS OF BILLIONAIRES, ICONS, AND, WORLD CLASS PERFORMERS.*

> "Borrow liberally, combine uniquely, and create your own bespoke blueprint."

MLT FRAMEWORK MINDMAP

A MINDMAP OF THE 15 PROCESSES OF THE MLT FRAMEWORK

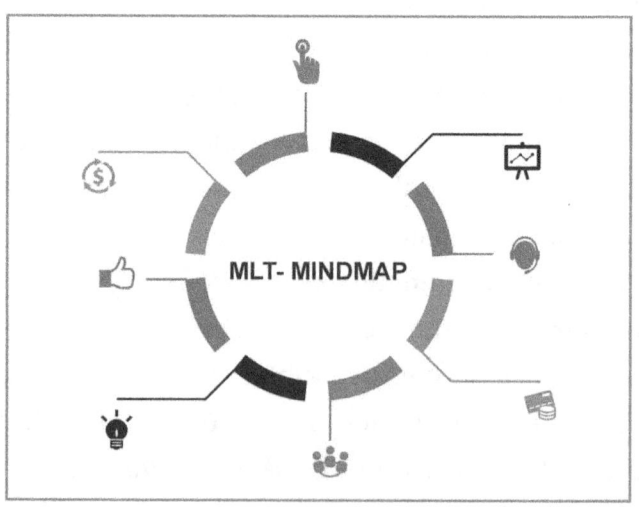

Visit the below link to get free bonus.
http://www.p3alphaconsulting.com/bonus/

www.ingramcontent.com/pod-product-compliance
Lightning Source LLC
Chambersburg PA
CBHW071434180526
45170CB00001B/346